insight text guide

Kevin Foster

Every Man in This Village Is a Liar

Megan Stack

First published in 2014, reprinted in 2015, 2016.

Insight Publications Pty Ltd
3/350 Charman Road
Cheltenham VIC 3192
Australia
Tel: +61 3 8571 4950
Fax: +61 3 8571 0257
Email: books@insightpublications.com.au

www.insightpublications.com.au

National Library of Australia Cataloguing-in-Publication entry:
Foster, Kevin, author.
Megan Stack's Every man in this village is a liar / Kevin Foster.
9781922243294 (paperback)
Insight text guide.
Includes bibliographical references.
For secondary school age.
Stack, Megan K. Every man in this village is a liar.
Stack, Megan K.—Criticism and interpretation.
956.054

Other ISBNs:
9781925175097 (digital)
9781925175424 (bundle: print + digital)

Cover design: The Modern Art Production Group

Printed in Australia.

contents

CHARACTER MAP

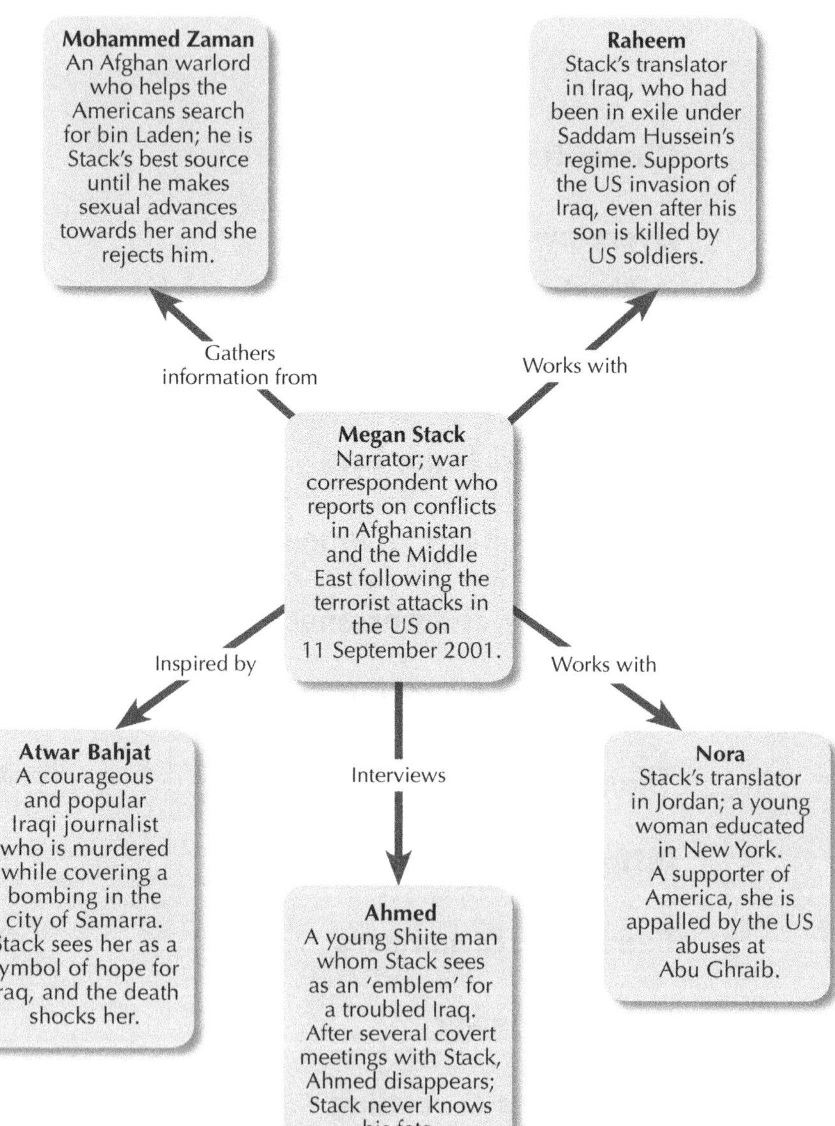

OVERVIEW

About the author

Megan Stack was born in Glastonbury, Connecticut, in 1975. She is a Pulitzer Prize–nominated journalist who writes for the *Los Angeles Times*. Formerly the newspaper's Houston bureau chief, Stack was catapulted into life as a foreign correspondent following the September 11 attacks. When the hijacked aircraft hit the World Trade Center towers, she was visiting her sister in Paris. Unlike her colleagues, who were grounded by the closure of US airspace, she was free to travel. Within weeks she was in Afghanistan, where her great adventure, and the education in war that it brought, began.

Over the next six years, as the war on terror took shape and widened in scope, Stack chased its outbreaks and reverberations across more than twenty countries in the Middle East, Central Asia, North Africa and the Arabian Peninsula. She reported from theocracies (countries ruled by religious leaders) and dictatorships (countries ruled by one person who has absolute power), their people frightened into conformity or terrorised into passivity. She encountered nations seething with rebellion, and others deadened by indifference; she witnessed countries in chaos, and societies in freefall.

Over time, the accumulation of horrors took its toll on Stack, and she looked for a posting away from the war zone. In 2007, she accepted a post as *Los Angeles Times* bureau chief in Moscow. Free from the daily round of battle, bombing and trauma, Stack found the critical distance to begin looking back through her notebooks, organising the memories and reflections that became *Every Man in This Village Is a Liar*. Published in 2010, the book, her first, was a non-fiction finalist in that year's US National Book Awards. In the same year, Stack took up a new role as chief of the *Los Angeles Times'* Beijing bureau. She is married to fellow foreign correspondent Tom Lasseter.

Synopsis

Every Man in This Village Is a Liar deals with real people and events. Stack recounts her experience of reporting on the US-led invasion of Afghanistan in the wake of the September 11 attacks, and on the invasion of Iraq, with the virtual civil war this unleashes. She also describes reporting on the conflict between Israel and its enemies up to the Israeli incursion into Lebanon in 2006, a rigged election in Egypt, insurgency in Yemen, the threat of terror in Saudi Arabia, life under dictatorship in Libya, and more.

In one sense this is a deeply personal book. It traces Stack's journey as a correspondent – from fresh-faced ingenue to embittered old hand – as she comes to better understand the reasons for and effects of US intervention in the region, while chronicling the emotional and psychological damage that she experiences along the way. At the same time it is a highly political book, engaged with some of the major political questions of the day. How does one establish and maintain security? When is the use of force appropriate, and what principles should dictate its employment? How can one retain humanity in an inhuman environment?

It is difficult to give a synopsis for the book that doesn't just read as a list of the places from which Stack reports. What gives the narrative its impetus and carries the reader from chapter to chapter is its themes, particularly surrounding the war on terror: the war's agents, its victims, and its effects on the people of the region and on the United States. We accompany Stack as she travels through those countries directly under assault from the United States (Afghanistan and Iraq), those affected by the new political realities created by the war on terror (Israel and Lebanon), those threatened by the new order the war has inaugurated (Yemen and Saudi Arabia) and those that have profited from this (Egypt and Libya). These journeys regularly bring Stack back to the region's newest political and military quagmire, Iraq, and the site of its oldest and most intractable struggle, Israel's conflict with its neighbours. In both of these places she demonstrates that whatever America's rhetoric about remaking the Middle East, whatever its delusions of a new dawn for democracy and a new age of peace, its ambitions will be thwarted – bloodily.

In the prologue, Stack reaches back to a memory from her childhood: she tells us of a male relative who, as a member of the US Marines, had survived Islamic militant group Hezbollah's 1983 bombing of the Marine barracks in Beirut that killed around 250 men, but had taken his life some years later, after returning to the United States. The message that Stack extracts from this bleak event provides a key focus for her own experience of war, and an insight into the broader damage that is done to societies and their people by violence:

> the first thing I knew about war was also the truest, and maybe it's as true for nations as for individuals: You can survive and not survive, both at the same time. (p.4)

The book is, in one respect, a study of how societies that deploy deadly force and those caught in its path deal with the experience of invasion or assault, and what this process does to them. It considers how people subject to tyranny, oppression or terror adapt themselves to these conditions: how they live with the routine violation of their basic rights and the constant fear of arrest, torture or death; what, in the process, they are able to preserve of their identities, and what they lose. Centrally, Stack contemplates her own survival – what covering these wars has done to her as a person; what she has lost and gained; and where these experiences have left her.

Character summaries

Stack is the key character in the text. She comes into contact with a number of individuals, none of whom, with the exception of Raheem, appear in more than one chapter. Stack uses these figures to embody particular places, views or experiences; they are as much symbols or representations of certain attitudes and beliefs as they are characters.

Megan Stack

Stack is the one constant presence in the narrative. This is the story of her education in war. A youthful reporter when the book opens, her 'education' is less about the mechanics of war than it is about war's effects, her country and herself. (Indeed, for a book about 'war', it is notable how little actual fighting there is.) Her experiences take her from an innocent idealism about America's place and purpose in the world to a disillusioned realism about how it conducts itself and what effects this has. The twin narratives of personal journey and political analysis closely shadow each other: Stack's political insights are often arrived at through personal experience, while her analysis of a given situation averts our gaze from its effects on her. Though she is often guarded about how particular incidents have impacted upon her, by the closing chapters she is struggling to function, and at the book's conclusion she suffers a form of breakdown.

Mohammed Zaman

Zaman is an Afghan warlord newly returned to Afghanistan from exile after the years of Taliban rule. Zaman provides fighters in the search for Osama bin Laden; in return, he seeks arms and money from the Americans that he will use to claim a position of power in the new order emerging in the country. His past is shrouded in mystery: he is rumoured to be a heroin trafficker and a legendary fighter who killed his enemies with his bare hands. He is a wily, hardened survivor whose alliances are built on convenience, not principle. Stack relies on him for access to information on the hunt for bin Laden but later breaks with him.

Raheem

Stack's translator in Iraq, Raheem is a former teacher who spent many years in exile from Saddam Hussein's regime. Quiet, sober and dignified, he is a consummate professional, deeply committed to his job and the responsibilities it entails. He is a believer in the American intervention and the freedom it has brought to Iraq. Though his son is later shot and killed by American soldiers – a random victim of a careless military – Raheem retains a cautious but steadfast commitment to the possibilities of the new Iraq.

Nora

A young Jordanian woman educated in the United States, Nora accidentally becomes Stack's translator during her time in Amman. For girlish and privileged Nora, the demonstrations in Jordan subsequent to the US invasion of Iraq lend a frisson of participation in a greater cause without any of the inconveniences of sacrifice or significant danger. A believer in the idea of America, she is appalled by the photographs of American abuse at Abu Ghraib prison and articulates a broader dismay at America's failure to live up to its espoused ideals.

Atwar Bahjat

An Iraqi journalist, Bahjat was a television newsreader under Saddam's regime, later working as a war correspondent for news organisations Al-Jazeera and Al-Arabiya. A fearless witness to her country's descent into chaos, she did not identify with either of the main religious sects, Sunni or Shiite, but saw herself merely as an Iraqi. Embodying the 'mad hope' (p.195) for a better Iraq, her fate suggests just how delusional this hope was: she is murdered while covering the bombing of the Al-Askari mosque, one of the Shiites' holiest shrines, in Samarra.

Ahmed

Looking for a way to tell the story of a city (Baghdad) and a country (Iraq) descending into chaos, Stack seeks out a representative subject and finds Ahmed. A young Shiite, Ahmed lives on the margins, his perfect English wasted in a menial job, his physical frustrations expressed through his obsessive running. His involvement with Stack possibly leads him to a grisly end – we never know, and neither does she. Though Stack intends for Ahmed to be a symbol of thwarted Iraqi hope, he ends up embodying the costs of careless US involvement in Iraq.

BACKGROUND & CONTEXT

The events in the text take place in the Middle East, Central Asia, the Arabian Peninsula and North Africa, in the wake of the September 11 attacks on the United States and in the emerging political context of the war on terror.

September 11

On 11 September 2001, four US passenger aircraft were hijacked after taking off from airports on the country's east coast. Two of the planes were deliberately piloted into the North and South towers of the World Trade Center in New York. The ensuing explosions and fires brought both buildings to the ground. Another plane headed to Washington, where it hit the Pentagon, the symbolic heart of American military power, while a fourth crashed in a field in Pennsylvania when its passengers fought to overpower the hijackers.

These were the deadliest terrorist attacks on US soil in the nation's history: around 3000 people lost their lives, including the nineteen hijackers, most of whom were Saudi Arabian nationals. It soon became clear that the hijackers – or, more accurately, suicide bombers – were supporters of Al Qaeda, the international terrorist group led by Saudi recluse Osama bin Laden, and that the attacks had been organised and planned in Afghanistan, where bin Laden enjoyed the protection of the fundamentalist Taliban government. US President George W. Bush described the attacks as an act of war, and promised that those responsible for them would be hunted down and brought to justice in an ongoing 'war on terror' (a term Bush first used in a televised address on 20 September 2001). The attacks had a profound psychological impact on the United States, which suddenly felt itself vulnerable to assault.

The invasion of Afghanistan

A little more than three weeks after the September 11 attacks, on 7 October 2001, US and international forces, allied with Afghan rebel groups, led an assault on Afghanistan intended to remove the Taliban from power, smash the terrorist training camps that had thrived there and catch their main sponsor, Osama bin Laden. While the Taliban were swiftly defeated and its fighters killed or pushed back over the border into Pakistan, the hunt for bin Laden stretched out for weeks, as the Tora Bora caves in the country's mountainous eastern frontier were searched. In the end, bin Laden slipped away, and it would be another decade, some time after Stack's book was published, before the Americans tracked him down and killed him (in Abbottabad, Pakistan, in May 2011).

In Afghanistan, the Americans found that while getting into the country had been easy, navigating their way through its maze of regional, tribal and familial alliances and getting out again would be much harder. The Afghans used the Americans to jockey for power, neutralise their enemies and fight their battles for them. The Americans soon found they were out of their depth, embroiled in a conflict they did not fully understand.

Rendition

Though the Americans failed to catch their number-one target, many hundreds of terrorist suspects were captured, rounded up and sent to a hastily prepared detention camp on the US military base at Guantanamo Bay, in Cuba. Others were 'rendered' to third countries, many of which had a history of human-rights violations. Here, the authorities were given *carte blanche* to do whatever they had to in order to extract the requisite intelligence. Interrogation techniques not normally sanctioned by civilised societies, including stress positions (making individuals stand or crouch in positions that place stress on specific parts of the body), waterboarding (pouring water on the face, through a cloth) and more overt forms of torture, were employed against these victims of 'rendition' to extract information about past attacks and to prevent further operations. America, it was clear, was determined to capture and punish those responsible for the September 11 attacks, as well as their aiders and abettors. There was deep discomfort, both within and beyond the United States, that in sanctioning such excesses the nation was abandoning the high moral standards that it had long tasked other countries to uphold. Worse still, in pursuit of its enemies the United States was teaming up with some of the region's most notorious human-rights abusers and entrenching their power.

The invasion of Iraq

In 1991, US troops had been at the head of an international military coalition that had ousted the Iraqis from Kuwait after they had invaded and looted the country. With Iraq's military in flight back across the border, President George H. W. Bush (the father of George W. Bush) was urged to pursue them all the way to Baghdad and to remove the country's long-established despot, Saddam Hussein, from power. Though the Americans held back, they encouraged Iraqis to rise up and overthrow their dictator. When Shiite (an Islamic sect) and Kurdish (an ethnic group inhabiting Kurdistan) militias did so, initiating revolts in the north and south of the country, the Americans failed to come through with promised military assistance, and the uprisings were crushed. For the next decade, Hussein's governing Baath Party ruthlessly oppressed its religious and ethnic foes, and impeded the international community's efforts to dismantle or destroy the country's arsenal of chemical and biological weapons.

In the wake of the September 11 attacks, George W. Bush accused the Iraqis of sponsoring terror and of having links with Al Qaeda, and made it clear that he was preparing to finish the job his father had left undone.

Over the next fourteen months, a relentless campaign of propaganda, persuasion and, on occasions, outright falsehood prepared the public for an invasion of Iraq. It was ostensibly to be undertaken to locate and dismantle Iraq's weapons of mass destruction.

The invasion of Iraq began on 20 March 2003, when a coalition of troops from the United States, Britain, Australia and Poland pushed north from their bases in Kuwait, fighting a series of battles on their way up to Baghdad. When the Iraqi capital fell on 9 April, the conventional military phase of the war was over. Yet the end of this stage of the fighting marked the beginning of the real struggle in Iraq. The fall of the dictatorship brought an almost complete breakdown in law and order, the chaos enhanced by the US decision to disband the country's only sources of authority, the army and the police force.

In the following weeks, government ministries, shops, museums and homes were looted and destroyed, old scores were settled and the only law in force was the law of the gun. Religious divisions between two Islamic sects – the minority Sunnis, who had prospered under Saddam's rule, and the majority Shiites, who had suffered – became the fault line along which the nation split. The streets became a killing ground. Sunni death squads targeted Shiites, and Shiite militias pursued revenge attacks. Nobody was safe. Al Qaeda and other terrorist groups exploited the chaos. Car bombs and suicide attacks became a daily occurrence across the country, and thousands of civilians lost their lives. Increasingly, US soldiers were the target of improvised explosive devices (IEDs), ambushes and other armed assaults. From 2003 to 2006, when Stack was reporting from Iraq, the country moved to the brink of civil war and dissolution.

Libya and Yemen

The war on terror changed the political landscape in the Middle East, North Africa and the Arabian Peninsula. Where the United States had once lectured despotic regimes in the region on human rights and democracy, its actions in Afghanistan and particularly in Iraq made it clear that no tyrant, however firm his grip on power at home, was safe any more. Saddam had been deposed not because of his disrespect for human rights, or even his alleged possession of weapons of mass destruction, but because he would not bend to the will of the United States. In the new order, regimes would accede to America's demands or risk retaliation.

At the same time, the Americans needed their former enemies to flush out the terrorists who had sought sanctuary in these countries. The security apparatus that the despots had used to track, terrorise and torture their own people could now be employed identifying, detaining and extracting intelligence from America's enemies. As a result of these new alliances of convenience, some of the region's most notorious sponsors of terror, Libya and Yemen, bought themselves back into favour with the United States by acknowledging US power and taking on its dirty work.

Adventures in democracy

Flush with its successes in Afghanistan and Iraq, the United States envisioned the overthrow of dictatorships and the spread of democracy throughout the region. However, despite its tireless proselytising for the ballot box, the United States was not always pleased by the results it delivered. Elections in the Occupied Territories of Israel and a ballot in Lebanon produced sizeable votes for extreme Islamist organisations. By the time Egypt went to the polls in 2005, America's enthusiasm for democracy was waning. As the only credible opposition to the repressive Mubarak regime came from the region's largest Islamic organisation, the Muslim Brotherhood, the Americans were content to look the other way while Mubarak brazenly stole the election. Just as the war had led America into a range of uncomfortable political affiliations, so it brought it to the discomforting rationalisation that democracy did not always serve its best interests.

Israel and the Palestinians

The Israeli–Palestinian conflict is the catalyst for much of the violence in the Middle East. The source of deep international resentment towards the United States, it is the region's longest-running dispute: so long-running that to give a brief history is impossible. For the purposes of Stack's text, the key issues relate to Israel's occupation of Palestinian land on the West Bank and along the Gaza Strip after the Six-Day War in June 1967, Israel's construction of settlements for its people on this land, and the Palestinians' longstanding efforts to reclaim this lost territory and establish a separate Palestinian state. These efforts have moved in and out of conference rooms and on and off the streets; negotiations have failed, and bombs and bullets have been no more successful.

In the early 1990s, the Oslo Accords seemed set to finally resolve the dispute. The accords, signed by Israeli Prime Minister Yitzhak Rabin and the chairman of the Palestinian Liberation Organisation, Yasser Arafat, provided for the withdrawal of the Israeli military and the creation of the Palestinian National Authority, through which the Palestinians would enjoy self-government in the West Bank and the Gaza Strip. However, a failure of mutual trust, provocative acts by both sides and the assassination of Prime Minister Rabin led to the breakdown and abandonment of the accords and a return to violence. The collapse of the Oslo Accords saw the further rise of extremist parties in the Palestinian territories, and the emergence of Sunni Islamic organisation Hamas as the major militant and political force in Gaza. To Israel's north, Hezbollah, Lebanon's Iranian-backed Shiite militia, in sympathy with the plight of the Palestinians, carried the fight to Israel, resulting in the major war that marks the final chapters of *Every Man in This Village Is a Liar*.

GENRE, STRUCTURE & LANGUAGE

Genre

Stack's text explicitly advertises its genre, a form of *bildungsroman*, through its subtitle, 'An Education in War'. A *bildungsroman* traces the early growth of a central character. *Every Man in This Village Is a Liar* fits this genre as it offers a description of the narrator's education and youthful development, and the process by which maturity is achieved.

Stack's identity is shaped powerfully by the experiences of war and its attendant sufferings. Yet for much of this text, these sufferings are not a central focus. While we experience events from Stack's perspective, for the greater part of the book she draws a veil over how particular experiences affect her; instead, she shifts the focus onto others and reads the wars through the effects on them. It is only when she heads towards a breakdown in the final chapters that we see the damage she has registered in others has mirrored her own, and that what we have been offered has been a referred accounting of the injuries she has sustained.

Every Man in This Village Is a Liar belongs within the tradition of the New Journalism, a style of news writing that emerged in the 1960s. In their non-fiction writing, the New Journalists – Ken Kesey, Tom Wolfe, Truman Capote, Joan Didion, Gay Talese, Norman Mailer and others – used techniques more readily associated with fiction, in an effort to render deeper truths about the issues with which they engaged: drugs, crime, sex, power, war. New Journalism was deeply engaged, notable for its activist impulses, its investigative practices, its determination to expose concealed truths and its reformist agenda. The key text to which Stack's book might trace its ancestry is Michael Herr's *Dispatches* (1977), a visceral and at times hallucinatory insight into Herr's experiences of reporting on the Vietnam War. Herr's argument in *Dispatches* was that conventional journalism, obsessed with the reporter's traditional questions (who, what, when, where and why), was hopelessly ill-equipped to convey the experience of the war in Vietnam, let alone explain what it meant:

> Conventional journalism could no more reveal this war than conventional firepower could win it, all it could do was take the most profound event of the American decade and turn it into a communications pudding, taking its most obvious, undeniable history and making it into a secret history. (Herr 1977, p.175)

Herr recognised that any journalist hoping to capture the truth of a war that divided America domestically and debased it in the eyes of the world could not simply stand aside and report on the contrasting comments from the national capitals. The only way to get at the 'undeniable history' of this war was to abandon objectivity and immerse oneself in it. Instead of presuming to cover the war, Herr let the war cover *him* and wrote about what that felt like.

The conflicts in Afghanistan and Iraq have produced some notable works of non-fiction by journalists who, like Stack, spent an extended period in the region. Such books provide a more direct comparison for her work. They include Dexter Filkins' *The Forever War* (2008), David Finkel's *The Good Soldiers* (2009) and Sebastian Junger's *War* (2010). Stack's book is distinguished by its broader geographical compass, its more extended chronology and the fact that, as a woman, she has access to places and experiences denied to male reporters – as we see particularly in the sections about working in Saudi Arabia.

Structure

Every Man in This Village Is a Liar comprises seventeen chapters, a prologue and an epilogue. The broad geographical scope of the book informs its structure. As the war on terror unfolds, Stack traces the trajectory of American engagement from righteous vengeance in Afghanistan to hubris and nemesis in Iraq, where, bogged down and directionless, it presides over the disintegration of the country. That is to say, Stack describes the United States' strategic and moral decline from purposeful engagement to bewildered entanglement, from principled openness to compromised concealment. She bears witness to how, as the nation pursues its war on terror, it loses sight of the goals that had originally taken it to Afghanistan and is drawn ever deeper into the murky domestic politics of the region. The United States is made increasingly complicit with the outrages of the area's tyrants and oppressors.

In keeping with this, although the first two chapters are set in Afghanistan, the narrative never returns there. Over the succeeding fifteen chapters (excluding Chapter Three, set in the United States), the narrative, while it takes Stack as far west as Libya and as far south as Yemen, consistently circles back to its focal points: Iraq, and Israel's contested northern border, with five chapters on Iraq and four on Israel, Palestine and Lebanon. If Iraq represents the social and humanitarian catastrophe that the United States has created, Israel's borders and the Jewish state's ongoing struggles against Hezbollah to the north and the Palestinians to the west and the south represent the intractable enmities of the region that, whatever the hopes of crafting a new Middle East, the United States can do nothing to alter.

This idea of a great unravelling, a loss of centredness and a growing entropy (disorder), is reflected in the opening and closing images of the book. In the first, Stack is woken in the grey light of a Jalalabad dawn by the unwanted attentions of Afghan warlord Mohammed Zaman, who has crept into her room to confess his love for her. Careful not to offend him because he is her best source, she rejects his advances and, full of hope and excitement, heads out to cover the war. In the final chapter, Stack – older, wiser and divested of her illusions – breaks down in an Amman restaurant and returns to the 'sterilized womb of a hotel, with smooth sheets and satellite television and thick robes, with a heavy door that kept the world away' (p.245). It was '[c]lean and removed, like a little piece of America', and she 'stayed there all night, until morning came' (p.245). If her awakening in Afghanistan represents a symbolic birth into her new role and the new identity it brings, her bedtime preparations in Amman imply a ritual preparation for death, as she embraces sleep and the welcome oblivion that it affords.

At the heart of Stack's engagement with the structure of the text lies a representational contradiction that persistently preoccupies her. The greater part of the book is focused on political and social collapse: on war, civil strife and terror, and the chaos and dissolution they bring. As a reporter, Stack's primary responsibility is to find order amid the chaos, to impose a comprehensible framework on incomprehensible events, to tidy up the messy reality of civil war and aerial bombardment and serve it up to her readers in an ordered, digestible form. It is an irony that she is attuned to and with which she struggles for the whole of the text.

Language

Stack's language is notable for its concreteness. She demonstrates the journalist's ability to provide key information about an event or sketch an individual with economy, clarity and wit. Her description of Mohammed Zaman's unwanted attentions is an excellent case in point: '[H]is calloused old hand was stroking my hair, cupping my scalp, fingers dripping like algae onto my ears and cheeks' (p.5).

One of Stack's challenges is to take the reader into unfamiliar environments – countries whose histories, cultures and values may be alien or unsettling to us – and make them comprehensible, even familiar, within the space of a few pages. It is a challenge she rises to on every occasion. Whether we are in the Saudi Aramco compound in Saudi Arabia, a hall in Yemen where men are chewing qat, a nightclub in Libya, the Beirut home of Lebanon's assassinated Prime Minister, a bombed village or a basement in a psychiatric hospital, Stack guides us through these places and points out the salient details that bring the moment and the people who inhabit it to life.

The fantasy America of Saudi Aramco's oil-company enclave is hinted at in the description of the setting and the refreshments:

> 'I made iced tea.' Valerie slid a platter of homemade chocolate chip cookies and cranberry cake onto a low-slung coffee table and collapsed into a sofa. (p.126)

In the impoverished Yemeni village of Jerif, the men gather in the 'qat-chewing hall' (p.152) to recite and listen to poetry, their shoddy clothes offset by the brittle dignity that their weaponry, the symbol of their manhood, affords: 'Cheap sports coats covered the men's thobes [shirt-like garments]; pistols bristled from their hips, and curved, carved daggers lay against their guts' (p.154). In Beirut, Stack takes us among the mourners in Rafik Hariri's home and plugs into the barely restrained hysteria of grief and rage that pulses there:

> 'God raise them,' somebody called, and all the grief tamped down under polished skin and polite faces suddenly throbbed in the hall. Women wailed and bent, bodies wilting over the coffin. Men with steely hair and tailored suits thrashed the air with strings of prayer beads, dropped heads into hands, and keened. (p.160)

In each of these passages, the critical detail that brings the scene to life, that animates it, resides in one or two nouns or verbs. At Hariri's wake the women 'wailed and bent' – a mixture of the animate and the inanimate evoking the agonised contortions of grief.

CHAPTER-BY-CHAPTER ANALYSIS

Prologue

Summary: *Stack reflects on what drove her to cover the war on terror and where her experiences have left her.*

Looking back on almost ten years of killing and dying, Stack reflects that the US determination, in the wake of the September 11 attacks, to go out and 'tame all the wilderness of the world' was an instinctive response, 'a way for Americans to convince ourselves that we were still strong and correct' (p.3). With the benefit of retrospect, Stack surveys the damage this folly has done to the United States, to the affected nations in the Middle East and to her, and judges September 11 the beginning of a 'disastrous reaction' (p.3). On reflection, she realises that 'the war on terror never really existed' (p.3).

Chapter One: Every Man in This Village Is a Liar

Summary: *Newly arrived in Afghanistan, Stack finds that the political and military landscape is more complicated than she had anticipated, and the costs of access unexpectedly steep.*

Stack's journey begins in Afghanistan, where her association with Mohammed Zaman gives her the first inkling that however principled US intentions are in the country, the United States will be sucked into, re-shaped and corrupted by the complex alliances that have moulded the nation's history. A ruthless opportunist, Zaman is a fitting emblem for the corrupted, old world to which America has tied its fortunes. He embodies the contradictions of Afghanistan: its deep charm and its unmistakable aura of menace. Intoxicated by the exoticism of her posting, Stack is at the same time disconcerted: not by the sudden proximity of death, but by the hollowness of her response to it. Over the course of her narrative, she will pass from feeling nothing to an unbearable excess of feeling, a hyper-sensitivity to her own vulnerability that ultimately drives her out of the war zone.

Stack's induction into the political rhetoric of the war occurs after US Defense Secretary Donald Rumsfeld denies her reports of the US destruction of the village of Kama Ado. In a place and a time where nothing is certain, facts are endlessly disputable, nobody can be trusted and 'Every man ... is a liar' (p.9), Stack begins to realise that in the new reality of the war on terror, truth is no longer an absolute but the servant of political necessity.

Q How are Stack's naivety and disorientation made clear in this chapter?

Q What does Stack's response to the news of the killing of her fellow correspondents imply about her?

Chapter Two: Chasing Ghosts

Summary: *Up in the mountains, the enemy and the men supposedly hunting them down seem to melt away in the thin air. Nothing here is certain. Down in the towns, Afghanistan's women live in seclusion and restriction – unaffected by the liberation America's invasion has supposedly brought to them.*

Though the Afghans are America's proxies in the fight against bin Laden's men in the hills on the Pakistan border, it is unclear whether there is greater antagonism towards the enemy or between the allies. Deals are made, alliances and tribal bonds are exploited, and nobody knows what accommodations have been arrived at with the enemy. This situation could hardly be further from the simple moral polarities that the Americans brought to the conflict, but in allying themselves with the Afghans, these are the new rules of the game. For Stack, this political problem manifests itself as a narrative challenge. No conventional narrative can convey the reality of a battle – if one is actually taking place – where friend is indistinguishable from foe, and the main target is as elusive as a ghost:

> [E]vents flickered, split, and rolled away like mercury. To write about the battle in an organized way, to shuffle the pieces, tap the sides, and square it into paragraphs and quotations was a fabrication. (p.28)

Down in Jalalabad, Afghanistan's women remain locked in a parallel world – despite the US conviction that America's invasion has liberated them. Trapped in the seemingly inescapable web of family and tradition, they are waiting for the sort of profound change that appears unlikely ever to come. Stack notes, 'These women had been waiting in these dim rooms for years ... [T]he Taliban was gone, but so what? Still they waited for their world to change' (p.19). Intelligent and defiant, they make of their lives what they can, hardly daring to hope for something better.

Key point

From early in the book, Stack confronts the problem of narrative form. She regularly asks herself how she might best tell a story in a comprehensible, ordered way while remaining true to the chaos and disorder that it describes.

Q How does the high-flown rhetoric behind the war on terror compare to the ways in which it is actually fought?

Q How are Afghanistan's women affected by the changes sweeping the country? What are the compensations of their secluded world?

Chapter Three: As Long as You Can Pay for It

Summary: *Stack recognises how the September 11 attacks have changed America, fixating it on fear and vulnerability, and how her experiences in Afghanistan have changed her.*

When Stack returns to the United States, she finds 'a country transformed' (p.30) by the September 11 attacks. She is struck by the radical disconnect between Americans' sense of their victimhood and the nation's actual role as an aggressor overseas:

> People had begun to imagine the country as a place waiting to get hit, defined by impending violence. And yet there was the war. We were warriors abroad and victims at home, and it didn't add up to anything coherent. (p.33)

This sense of things not adding up is compounded by her realisation that while her experiences in Afghanistan have changed her, America has been so distorted by its experience that it has become alien to her – that though she is back in her country, she is 'still trying to get home' (p.31). While her grandfather, a World War II veteran, reassures her that she, and the country, will accommodate themselves to what they have endured, Stack realises that war has marked her irrevocably, and she will never find her way back to the settled certainties of old.

Q How do the politics of fear display themselves in America?

Q What insights about herself and the effects of her experiences does Stack glean from her conversation with her grandfather?

Chapter Four: Terrorism and Other Stories

Summary: *In Israel, Stack gets a glimpse of the moral peril that confronts America. Accustomed to living with the threat of terror, Israel struggles to maintain its moral compass, to exercise power justly and to acknowledge the humanity of the enemies with whom it fights and shares land.*

From a society newly terrorised by suicide attacks, Stack returns to the Middle East, to Israel, a nation long accustomed to such assaults and hardened by the experience. Here she sees that the exercise of force can do as much damage to those who inflict it as it does to those on its receiving end.

Like the Americans, the Israelis crave security, but they have mistaken power over the Palestinians for protection from them. The more the Palestinians resist, the more uncompromising Israel's response, and the more this demands that each regards the other as less than fully human. The Hasidic boys that Stack sees walking towards the Old City taunt and spit on the Palestinian man because they regard him as a lesser being. At the government level, these same assumptions underlie the seclusion of Palestinian prisoners to separate jails and their maltreatment and torture. To buy security with brute force is to pay for it with one's soul. The dilemmas that confront Israel are increasingly the dilemmas that confront America: how can a country administer power morally? How can it secure its people from its enemies and still preserve its humanity?

Key point

Power is a double-edged sword. When force is not employed morally or with restraint, it does almost as much damage to those who wield it as to those who bear its blows.

Key vocabulary

Hasidic: meaning 'the pious'; an Orthodox Jewish sect that stresses kindness, charity and religious enthusiasm.

Q How does the attack on the old Palestinian man by the Hasidic boys illuminate the broader political conditions of the country?

Q Explain how the tortured Palestinian woman's story – wounded by her torturer, comforted by her guard – reveals the moral complexities of the conflict in Israel.

Chapter Five: Forgive Us Our Trespasses

Summary: *Stack witnesses Baghdad descend into chaos as the US army overpowers the last of the Iraqi military, and the people break loose from decades of oppression in an orgy of violence, retribution and looting. She is conscious of how ill-equipped she or any journalist is to convey the magnitude of these events.*

Stack's next post is Iraq, in 2003, where the US invasion has removed Saddam Hussein and his regime, the Iraqi army and police force have been disbanded and there is no law, order or security. The war has transformed Baghdad from a sophisticated, modern city to something between a graveyard and a jungle, less a society than a theme park for vengeance and predation. As the bodies pile up at makeshift mortuaries, relatives pour in to claim them, and more bodies follow. Stack realises the folly and the essential dishonesty of her task as a journalist, expected to offer perky updates from a society in freefall:

> The invasion was a nasty, impersonal force, and people had been walloped. And me, pretending I could encapsulate it all in a few paragraphs, grabbing a quote from this victim or that, scribbling scraps of description. (p.60)

Q Re-read pages 57–9, as Stack describes Baghdad's descent into anarchy. What details does she draw on and which narrative techniques does she use to convey this downward spiral?

Chapter Six: The Living Martyr

Summary: *Newly liberated, Iraq's Shiites head to the city of Karbala for the Day of Ashura and to mourn their dead. Devotion and grief mix with shame as the enormity of what they have suffered under Saddam finds expression.*

The toppling of the dictator has lifted decades of restraint. The country is unhinged with grief and intoxicated with its new freedoms. With her translator, Raheem, Stack follows the multitude of Shiites heading to Karbala to celebrate the Day of Ashura. In Saddam's Sunni-dominated Iraq, Shiites had observed this ceremony in secret. Likewise, they had been compelled to mourn the loss of their loved ones, the victims of Saddam's terror, behind closed doors. Now they are able, for the first time in decades, to mourn their dead and celebrate their faith: 'Every Shiite wanted a taste of a pilgrimage that had been outlawed under Saddam' (p.64).

The pilgrimage to Karbala unleashes a torrent of repressed grief: 'Every family had scars, secret graves, people who got erased from the world ... Beneath [Imam Hussein's] overarching martyrdom, all the other martyrs took their place' (p.66). As Shiite Iraqis confront what Saddam's regime has done to them, the overwhelming sentiments are shame and a thirst for justice. Stack meets Hussein Safar, the 'living martyr' (p.74) who survived an execution squad, returned to indict the murderers and was killed for speaking out. Stack wonders how people who have been so damaged can restore themselves and reclaim their self-respect – what hope is there for Iraq?

Key vocabulary

Day of Ashura: one of the holiest days for Shiite Muslims. It celebrates the martyrdom of the Prophet Muhammad's grandson, Hussein, at Karbala. The day is marked by fasting, pilgrimage and ritual re-enactments of Hussein's suffering as men whip and cut themselves.

Shiite and *Sunni*: Islam's two main sects. Their division can be traced back to the martyrdom of Hussein.

Q What do we know about Raheem, based on Stack's description of her travels through Iraq with him? How does Stack convey this information to us? How does this information shape our view of him?

Q What does the story of Hussein Safar, the 'living martyr', reveal about life in Iraq under Saddam Hussein?

Chapter Seven: The Leader

Summary: *Stack travels to Libya, where Colonel Muammar Qaddafi is in power. Libya is a dictatorship, where people live in fear. It is also on the front lines in the war on terror, and a focus for the moral contradictions the United States is embracing in its pursuit of its enemies.*

Travelling from Iraq to Libya, 'backward in time, into the rogue dictatorship preserved under glass' (p.80), Stack gets a glimpse of what life would have been like in Iraq under Saddam Hussein. The people in Libya live in terror, struck dumb by fear; they watch every word and hastily backtrack from any hint of criticism of the government. While the United States justified Saddam's removal on the basis that he was 'an oppressor and a tyrant' (p.79), it tolerates or cooperates with Libya's notorious leader, Colonel Qaddafi, who is also known for human-rights abuses. Qaddafi proves to be a brilliant strategist who has used the war on terror to rehabilitate the most terror-friendly nation in the region and cement his power. Though Libya is no better than Iraq, the United States overlooks its excesses because it kowtows to American power and supports the war on terror.

Q What does Stack's experience of Libya reveal to her about what life was like in Iraq under Saddam Hussein?

Q How has Libya profited from the war on terror?

Chapter Eight: Sacrifice

Summary: *In Kurdistan, Stack sees the human reality behind the death tolls. She links the propensity for violence she finds in the region with the blind faith that so many profess. And though she makes every effort to keep herself unsullied, she knows that the stain of such violence will mark her.*

Back in Iraq, the country is breaking apart under the weight of sectarian violence. Stack experiences this most keenly on a trip to Mosul in 2004, where she goes to report on a series of bombings. While the bombs are detonated to make a political point, Stack, in visiting the hospitals where the injured are being tended to, is overwhelmed by their physical consequences: 'A suicide bomb is a political statement; it is intended that way. But it's hard to find politics in the particular' (p.99).

The explosions coincide with Eid al-Adha, the festival celebrating Ibrahim's preparedness, at the Lord's command, to sacrifice his son, Ishmael, and the child's last-minute reprieve. Stack sees in this story of blind faith a living principle that shapes the conduct of disputes in the Middle East and contributes to their take-no-prisoners politics: '[T]he Middle East is still packed with murderers who believe they are doing

God's will' (p.103). Attending a family celebration of Eid, Stack watches while a calf is slaughtered for a feast; as it bleeds to death, the children 'giggled and knelt down, poking their palms into the blood, playing with it' (p.105). The killing of the innocent here is not a cause for regret but a cultural rite, and though Stack vainly endeavours to keep the blood off her shoes, she gives up, knowing 'it would stain me, too' (p.105). So it goes in Iraq, where a rising tide of blood will leave its mark on Stack and on America as a whole.

Key vocabulary

Kurdistan: the parts of northern Iraq, Iran, Syria and the south-east of Turkey that are occupied by Kurds, a distinct ethnic group. In the post-Saddam period, the north of Iraq became the semi-autonomous region of Kurdistan.

Eid al-Adha: meaning 'feast of sacrifice', this is one of the most important festivals in the Muslim calendar. It celebrates Allah's command to Ibrahim that he sacrifice his son, and Ibrahim's readiness to do so.

Q Examine the scene in the hospital. What details does Stack fix on to convey the human toll behind the headlines?

Q How does Stack use the sacrifice of the calf to make a larger point about what is happening in Kurdistan and across the region?

Chapter Nine: We Expected Something Better

Summary: *In Jordan, Stack finds a place safely removed from the turmoil in Iraq and feigning indignation over the fate of its neighbour. Her friend Nora is disillusioned by revelations of torture in Abu Ghraib prison, while Stack struggles with her own dismay.*

In Amman, Jordan, Stack meets Nora, a manicured, US-educated twenty-something with an unconditional love for all things American. Nora and her fashion-conscious friends meet in chic cafes and pretend they live in a repressive state – they watch their tongues, speak in code and see spies in every corner. But, like Jordan as a whole, they are play-acting political engagement. Denouncing US intervention in Iraq, the Jordanians feign indignation, but – too comfortably removed from the bloody centres of resistance and rebellion, and too coddled to want to be where the real action is taking place – they can barely remember the basic grammar of protest.

The revelations of US torture at Abu Ghraib prison deeply dismay Nora: she had invested in 'the *idea* of America' (p.122) and is stricken when the reality falls short. Though Stack dismisses her complaints, she eventually recognises her own feeling of deflation in Nora's disappointment. America bears the unrealistic hopes of a world grown sick with brutality, compromise and failure. Triumphant in its commitment to freedom and human rights, the United States represents a universal aspiration towards something better, especially among those living under oppression. When America's conduct violates its ideals, as at Abu Ghraib, it is not only a national failing but also a blow to collective hope in other parts of the world.

Q What *did* Nora expect from the United States?

Q Why does Nora's disappointment so irritate Stack?

Chapter Ten: A Question of Cost

Summary: *In Saudi Arabia, Stack discovers the depth of American complicity with the kingdom's brutality and oppression, and recognises her place in that relationship.*

Though the Americans and the Saudis are 'braided together' by oil, their 'weird codependence' (p.128) is underpinned by mutual revulsion. Whatever the superficial comforts of the oil-company compounds, this makes for a hostile environment. Politics here is personal. The unchallenged authority of the nation's rulers trickles down through the state, replicating its inequalities of power at every level – most clearly revealing its true face in the relations between men and women. Saudi Arabia's women are trapped and dependent, either brainwashed, beaten or too thoroughly benefitting from the system to kick against it.

As a woman, Stack has direct experience of what it is like to be a second-class citizen, and she rails against the kingdom's restrictions. Yet she tolerates the indignities heaped upon her because she stands to profit from them: 'Like America itself, you have done a calculation, you have accepted a condition, because you wanted something out of it' (p.138). In this regard she is no different from the carefully coiffed housewives in the compounds. If they have sold their souls for a slice of 'the elusive American dream' (p.127), Stack has traded hers for an opportunity to write about them.

Key point

Though the United States promotes itself as the defender of democratic freedoms, it is prepared to overlook human-rights violations where its strategic or business interests are at stake. Lofty principles rarely survive an encounter with the political and economic demands of the real world. Compromise is a deflating fact of life for nations, as much as for the individuals who inhabit them.

Q Why are the United States and Saudi Arabia 'braided together'?

Q What does this co-dependence reveal to Stack about her country?

Chapter Eleven: Loddi Doddi, We Likes to Party

Summary: *In Yemen, Stack discovers an emblem of how America's pursuit of the war on terror has led it into alliances with people it cannot understand or hope to control.*

If Saudi Arabia was awash with uncomfortable truths about US complicity in repression, in Yemen Stack finds it almost impossible to confirm anything. Chaperoned by government officials, steered through anodyne or promotional interviews, she struggles to penetrate the mask of falsehood. Where human-rights lawyers had once turned to the United States for assistance, the nation is now the chief suspect in abuses, rendering extremists to Yemeni authorities: as one lawyer tells Stack, 'The governments in the Arab and Islamic world work as police stations now for the United States' (p.147). Political repression meets with tribal tradition in the chewing of qat: the whole country is half-stoned, embracing its cultural heritage while seeking escape from its present-day hardships into oblivion. Beyond the security bubble of its capital, Sanaa, Yemen is the Wild West of the Middle East – untamed, and, in the north, where a rebellion is raging, seemingly ungovernable.

It is in partaking in the tribal customs of Yemen at a poetry recital that Stack comes closest to hearing the unfiltered truth about the country. Here the men rail against the arrogance of the West, denounce the Israelis, decry the spinelessness of their leaders and lament the erosion of the country's traditions. A strategic ally in the war on terror, Yemen cannot conceal its aversion to Western values.

Key vocabulary

Qat: an evergreen plant whose leaves are chewed as a stimulant.

Q 'There was so much lying and hiding going on that you couldn't believe much of anything unless you saw it yourself' (p.152). What is Stack able to learn about what the United States is doing in Yemen from what she sees?

Chapter Twelve: A City Built on Garbage

Summary: *In Lebanon, Stack finds a country that has never come to terms with its recent history of violent civil strife. The assassination of the Prime Minister threatens to split the country along the fault lines of religion and politics.*

Stack arrives in Beirut in February 2005 to report on the assassination of Prime Minister Rafik Hariri and its consequences for Lebanon. Hariri's murder tips the country, still riven by a bitter civil war that destroyed it in the 1970s and 1980s, back towards destruction. While Christians, Druze and Sunnis pour into Martyrs' Square and declare a revolution against Syrian interference in Lebanese affairs, the minority Shiites, who have benefitted from Syrian domination, are conspicuous by their absence. When hundreds of thousands march to declare their loyalty to Syria, it becomes clear that nothing in Lebanon has changed. The country is still divided into bitterly antagonistic factions: 'Each side saw its own extinction in the alternate vision. They weren't living in the same country anymore; they had become divided until they couldn't even recognize one another' (p.170).

Key vocabulary

Druze: a minority religious sect most populous in Lebanon and Syria.
Hezbollah: meaning 'the party of God'; a Lebanese Shiite militia group and political party backed by Syria and Iran, in open conflict with Israel.

Q How does Stack convey the repressed hysteria in Hariri's house prior to the funeral?

Q What does the story about West Beirut's garbage dump suggest about the state of contemporary Lebanon?

Chapter Thirteen: The Earthquake Nobody Felt

Summary: *In Egypt, the United States' support for fledgling democracies runs headfirst into its war on terror and the rise of Islamic fundamentalism via the ballot box.*

Where the Lebanese have been abandoned by the United States, Egypt, a loyal ally in the war on terror and a bastion against Islamic extremism, retains US support. Ironically, this support is cemented by the United States' growing disillusionment with democracy in the Middle East, where elections have returned an array of Islamist governments. There is little danger of that happening in Egypt's 2005 election. The only credible opposition to the Mubarak government comes from the Muslim Brotherhood, who, to the United States, represent the popular face of Islamic fundamentalism.

In the small town of Damanhour, Stack comes to understand the basis of the Brotherhood's power and popularity. The people gathered to hear its candidate are not the 'ragtag army of aging labor leaders, embattled human rights workers, scruffy bloggers, and rheumy professors' who populate the demonstrations in Cairo, but ordinary people, 'factory workers, farmers, and fathers ... women, too' (p.179). Stack notes, 'They rallied to the Islamists who came from their towns and mosques because they felt at home with them and recognized in their piety a reflection of their own moral values' (p.179). The election is a farce, and when the people protest they are set upon, tear-gassed and chased off the streets. Stack is beaten by government thugs and left seething with impotent fury, briefly experiencing what it is to be an Egyptian. Her rage is compounded by the fact that this despotism can only survive on the back of financial and moral support from the United States.

Key vocabulary

Muslim Brotherhood: a pan-Islamic religious, political and social movement. Vehemently anti-Western, it sees the Koran as the basis of legal and social organisation.

Q Who supports the Muslim Brotherhood in Damanhour, and why?

Q Why, according to Stack, are the Americans prepared to turn a blind eye to the subversion of democratic process described in this chapter?

Chapter Fourteen: All Things Light, and All Things Dark

Summary: *The fate of Atwar Bahjat embodies Iraq's collapse into sectarian slaughter and the extinguishment of any last, mad hope that a modern, secular Iraq might arise out of the rubble of Saddam Hussein's regime.*

Back in Iraq, Stack is shocked by the death of Iraqi journalist Atwar Bahjat, murdered while covering the bombing of Samarra's Al-Askari mosque, one of the Shiites' holiest shrines, in February 2006. While she lived, Bahjat bridged the divide between old and new Iraq. A television newsreader during Saddam's reign, dispensing state propaganda, she became a poet, novelist and respected war correspondent. The product of a mixed marriage, 'a theological half-breed' (p.196), she had no sect, and placed her faith in Iraq.

Bahjat's death is important because, as a public figure, her pointless slaughter gives citizens a means to articulate the anger and despair rising up from the hundreds of thousands of anonymous deaths. Stack sees in Bahjat a 'mad hope for an impossible, alternative Iraq: a place of liberated men and women, and the free exchange of ideas; a society that had moved beyond its sectarian differences' (p.195). If Bahjat's life embodied the hope for a better Iraq, so her death reflects the failure of this hope. The responses of Bahjat's colleagues at Al-Arabiya give Stack a new appreciation of what it means to be a reporter. For American journalists, the war is a series of challenges – to describe a given day's events before they move on to their next assignment. For Iraqis, national history is unfolding under their feet. They have a duty to tell this story, although they have to flirt with death to do so.

Q Trace the development of Atwar Bahjat's career, from newsreader under Saddam Hussein's regime to war reporter in the new Iraq, and explore how its progress reflects the changes in the country.

Chapter Fifteen: There Would Be Consequences

Summary: *Stack's attempts to tell the story of Iraq's slide into chaos through the experiences of a young Shiite has potentially tragic consequences. This brings her to the realisation that what for her is a narrative challenge, a problem of form and perspective, is for others a matter of life and death.*

Back in Baghdad in the summer of 2006, as Iraq tears itself asunder, Stack goes 'looking for a young Shiite, somebody whose life and aspirations and circumstances could serve as an emblem for a tortured land' (p.203). At Baghdad University she finds Ahmed, limbering up for a run. Raised on the social margins, his father a victim of political trouble, Ahmed has 'the face of a man who is learning, bit by bit, the limitations of empty pockets and lowly family stature' (p.204). The running that had once expressed his hope has become an exercise in futility, forever bringing him back to where he started – poor, trapped and frustrated.

Stack cannot go to Ahmed's house, nor can he come to her office – to do either would be to invite a death sentence. So they meet in the cafe at the Baghdad Hotel. Here, over a series of meetings, she learns his story. The better she comes to know him, the less he serves her purpose as a symbol. He is too thoroughly corporeal, too himself to be an emblem of anything other than his own hopes and vulnerabilities. After his girlfriend is recognised at the hotel one day by somebody from one of the militias, Ahmed's phone goes dead. Stack does not ever find out what happened to him. Guilt-stricken, she realises that what for her was a story is for him a matter of life and death; that her blithe and possibly fatal interference in Ahmed's life mirrors US indifference to the harm done by its intervention in Iraq. It is she, not Ahmed, who has become a symbol.

Q Describe how Ahmed feels about the state of his country and outline his hopes for the future. Be sure to cover his relationship with Stack, how it serves him and what he gets out of it.

Chapter Sixteen: Killing the Dead

Summary: *Stack journeys south into Lebanon during the Lebanon War of 2006. For Stack, this is a descent into hell: an objective hell of smashed cities, flattened towns and slaughtered innocents, and a personal hell of professional collapse.*

In July 2006, Hezbollah and Israel go to war. Israel's bombing campaign – justified as part of the war on terror – is intended to punish the whole country for Hezbollah's transgressions. Heading south, Stack comes under bombardment for the first time, and the facade of cool detachment that has seen her through her earlier experiences suddenly cracks. To Stack, crossing the Litani River is like crossing the

Acheron, the river in Greek mythology that marks the border between the lands of the living and the dead.

In the Palestinian refugee camp at Tyre, Stack finds the people raging and defiant, preparing to bury the scores of victims from the bombing. The Israelis and the Americans say that they want to 'destroy' Hezbollah, but the funeral reveals the futility of this goal:

> Hezbollah is rooted inside these people, in their houses and neighbourhoods and bellies. The more people you kill, unless you kill all of them, the stronger Hezbollah will live in the ones who remain. (p.226)

The dead live on through the living. The hospital at Tibnin is like a scene from Dante's journey through hell: the blackened basements are packed with desperate refugees, reduced, in the darkness, to disembodied voices of fear and suffering. Here the madness of the war finds human form. The town of Bint Jbeil has been pulverised by the air force, although when the bombardment slackens, Stack notes: 'A miracle is stirring. The broken, vanished town is full of Lazaruses' (p.235). The old and handicapped emerge from the wreckage, bloodied and babbling, 'staggering into the half-light' (p.235). The dead arise. These pathetic victims and their smashed houses are, Stack realises, the true face of the war on terror. The torment all around her echoes Stack's growing realisation that she has been lucky to last this long, but that she is now living at the very extremity of her nerves and is, unquestionably, heading for a crash: 'I know when this is over it will be like dying' (p.230).

Q How does Stack's description of the mass burial crystallise her views about the futility of trying to 'exterminate' one's enemies?

Q Discuss the classical idea of Hades (or the journeys of Dante, if you'd prefer). Consider how Stack's description of her journey south into Lebanon, towards the hospital at Tibnin and the ruined village of Bint Jbeil, draws on classical images of the passage to hell.

Key point

The war on terror is intended to stamp out fundamentalism and make the world safer for the United States and its allies. Yet the tactics by which it is pursued have the opposite effect: injustice breeds radicalisation, and terror begets further terror. Instead of eradicating extremism, the war on terror creates the perfect conditions for its extension.

Chapter Seventeen: I Thought I Was a Salamander

Summary: *Stack comes to recognise the damage that she has done to herself over the preceding five years, and in that process she recognises the damage that America's pursuit of security has visited on the region and its people.*

In the book's final chapter, Stack is still cowering under Israeli bombs in the south of Lebanon, struggling to be functional: 'I am too nervous to talk. I am jumping out of my skin' (p.237). In this state, she finds a psychiatric hospital abandoned by all but its patients. Here she has a series of encounters that clarify for her the truth about the war on terror: the sort of thinking that produced it, where this has led America and where it has left her. Lebanon isn't the only place where the lunatics have taken over the asylum. Stack realises that she has been able to get by to this point only by making herself 'tougher and smaller' (p.240). By retreating into her shell, she found: 'You can be anywhere if you're not really there' (p.240). In this radical detachment from the here and now, Stack sees the link between herself and her country. She had identified at the outset of the book as 'extremely American' (p.3) and now she realises how true this is:

> It occurs to me now that maybe this is the most American trait of all, the trademark of these wars. To be there and be gone all at once, to tell ourselves it just happened, we did what we did but we had no control over the consequences. (p.240)

Stack sees that though there may once have been a purpose to the war on terror in the immediate aftermath of September 11 – to catch bin Laden and to try to secure America from terror – it has descended into one purposeless slaughter after another, in search of a sense of security that no amount of killing can ensure:

> [U]p close the war on terror isn't anything but the sick and feeble cringing in an asylum, babies in shock, structure smashed ... And all along, America dreaming its deep sweet dream, there and not there. America chasing phantoms, running uphill to nowhere in pursuit of a receding mirage of absolute safety. (pp.242–3)

Q What, in your opinion, precipitates Stack's final breakdown?

Q What is the significance of Stack's reference to the salamander, and how does she employ it as an image in this chapter?

Epilogue

Summary: *Stack reflects on the death of Raheem's son and how this has affected him, and her.*

Raheem's son is killed by US soldiers, and his death becomes an emblem of the damage done by the United States in Iraq and throughout the region. Clumsy and careless, they have ruined untold lives, and for what gain? Raheem's response lends the book's conclusion a sliver of hope: abandoning his plans to leave for the United States, he commits himself to Iraq's uncertain future.

CHARACTERS & RELATIONSHIPS

The narrative focuses on the relationships through which Stack comes to experience and understand the places she visits or the conflicts she witnesses. Accordingly, Stack sits at the centre of all significant relationships in this book. None of the characters have relationships with other characters independent of her.

In many cases, the people who illuminate her understanding of life in an alien land barely constitute 'characters'. The book is littered with such figures: the doctor from the Libyan–American Friendship Association; the party guest in Tripoli, his tongue loosened by drink, who begs Stack that she report nothing he said and insists that they never met; the old woman in Karbala, finally able to openly mourn the daughter murdered by the government in the early 1980s, and many more. Stack's encounters with others work to round out or deepen her understanding of a particular place, and so progress the narrative.

Megan Stack

Key quotes

'As it turned out, the first thing I knew about war was also the truest, and maybe it's as true for nations as for individuals: You can survive and not survive, both at the same time.' (p.4)

'Like America itself, you have done a calculation, you have accepted a condition, because you wanted something out of it.' (p.138)

'You can be anywhere if you're not really there. You can walk into any room, drive down any road, ask any question, write about anybody's pain. You tell yourself you are unscathed. You stand smooth and count yourself unaffected.' (p.240)

Stack's journey takes her from a romantic vision of the foreign correspondent's lot to a cynical detachment about its demands and rewards, from single-minded professionalism to a shocked realisation about where her capacity for cold calculation might lead, from psychological wholeness to damage and partial collapse. Underlying all other journeys is her progress towards the realisation of her vulnerability – her passage through the valley of the shadow of death teaches her that the shadow, once felt, will never leave her.

Soon after Stack arrives in Afghanistan, the first Western journalists in the country are killed by the Taliban. She is shocked by the fact that the news leaves her feeling 'empty'; though she knows that she should feel empathy, she is 'gaping like a canyon' (p.8). One of the reasons she feels nothing is because death still seems distant and unreal to her. While the Afghans are accustomed to its presence and less inclined to regard its visitations as exceptional – Stack notes that in Afghanistan, 'Death was everywhere ... Afghans lived on the edge of mortality' (p.14) – Stack is never able to match this degree of indifference.

Though Stack is able to do her job in appalling circumstances and maintain an appearance of detachment, her humanity, and the vulnerability it affirms, asserts itself at unexpected moments – most notably when she faints in the Mosul hospital while interviewing the victims of a suicide bombing. By the time she arrives in southern Lebanon, where the Israelis are raining bombs on the region, her detachment has evaporated. Under bombardment, whatever her professional responsibility to record and interpret, she cannot help but regard herself as a target and a victim, and she begins to unravel. If Stack's task has been to bear witness to the war on terror and its effects on those caught up in it, she accomplishes this mission most effectively by becoming one of its victims. Unlike all but a handful of her fellow citizens, she knows what it is to be on the receiving end of pitiless military power: she knows what it is to be a target, to be innocent but counted guilty. She has walked in the victim's shoes, and though she has survived the experience, a part of her will never recover.

Mohammed Zaman

Key quotes

> 'He was an enemy of the Taliban, funded by the U.S. government, making a play for power in the vague, new order that had begun when American soldiers toppled the Taliban government. I was a stranger here, and he was my best source.' (pp.5–6)
>
> 'His calloused old hand was stroking my hair, cupping my scalp, fingers dripping like algae onto my ears and cheeks.' (p.5)
>
> 'The warlords plotted tribal revenge, scrapped for control of the heroin trade, lined their pockets and trolled for power. They tossed enemies into moldy jail cells, and sold them to the Americans who were rounding up jihadis. If you asked them why, they'd smile in chilling self-satisfaction and say, "He's a terrorist." Maybe it was true, and maybe it wasn't.' (p.10)

The first person we encounter in the book, the Afghan warlord Mohammed Zaman, exemplifies how Stack fashions her secondary characters with an eye to their symbolic value. As Zaman pads into the room where Stack sleeps, we are presented with a symbolic encounter between the United States and Afghanistan. The Americans have arrived in Afghanistan as the vanguard of a morally principled force: outraged by the attacks on their territory and citizenry, they are determined to track down those responsible and exact a righteous vengeance. Yet in coming to Afghanistan, the Americans have arrived in a place where the basic moral polarities that underpin their crusade – good against evil, the courageous against the cowardly, the modern against the medieval – do not apply. Afghanistan is an older, infinitely more complex political, social and moral space. Shaped by centuries of war, it is a country where matters of principle are contingent on the imperatives of survival, where alliances count only as long as they are useful and where what one says is not necessarily what one means. Both Zaman and Afghanistan are the ideal embodiments of the Epimenides paradox that gives the book its title:

> [It was] named after the Cretan philosopher who declared, "All Cretans are liars." It's one of the world's oldest logic problems ... If he's telling the truth, he's lying. If he's lying, he's telling the truth. That was Afghanistan after September 11. (p.9)

Stack soon realises that the simple categories of truth and falsehood have no currency in Afghanistan; that what somebody proffers as a fact or a lie is not necessarily either. In Afghanistan, truths reveal falsehoods while falsehoods conceal deeper truths. The only truth, Stack soon realises, is that there are no simple truths: 'Afghanistan was meaning washed away' (p.9).

As Zaman creeps into Stack's room, it is clear that the moral decency that the Americans had brought with them to Afghanistan is under assault. Zaman is a fitting emblem for the questionable, corrupted society to which America has inextricably tied its fortunes. Part oriental exotic, part conman, he embodies the contradictions of Afghanistan: its charm and its aura of danger. When Stack finally leaves his house after he protests his love for her, she is cast adrift in Afghanistan, left to find her own way in a complex, perilous environment. It's hard to know whether she's better or worse off without his help.

Raheem

Key quotes

'[H]e, for one, was willing to take the great mad gamble, because he'd concluded that any risk was better than Saddam Hussein. Why not try, said his posture and his quick, sharp glances.' (p.69)

'Back then the future looked clean and good, and Raheem was full of simple hope – that he and his sons would find stable jobs because Saddam was gone. I've never seen him so happy again.' (p.249)

Stack's Iraqi translator, Raheem, is the one character, apart from Stack, who makes more than a single appearance. In that regard, he is a figure of some significance. Always well-presented and professional, Raheem is 'discreet, perceptive, skilled at getting information out of people without letting them realize they'd given it' (pp.66–7). Raheem honed his skills as an adroit interpreter of the environment while resisting Saddam's dictatorship. His refusal to join the ruling Baath Party condemned him and his family to danger, economic hardship and long periods of separation. Lucky to survive ten years in the army, he was forced to pursue a teaching career overseas in order to support his family back in Iraq. In this sense, he too was a victim of Saddam.

Raheem accepts the upheavals that follow the toppling of Saddam, refusing to condemn the disorganisation and danger that ensue. The war uncorks the optimist in him: when he looks around, he sees not social and economic disorder but a nation making itself anew. In his noble, principled professionalism, his reserve and his deep inner warmth, Raheem embodies the best of Iraq that Saddam's terror decimated or drove overseas, but never extinguished.

The quality that Stack most admires in Raheem is his loyalty. Even when 'the war slithered into his house and broke his heart for good', he 'never sold the Americans out' (p.69). What Stack is alluding to here is the personal tragedy that visits Raheem's family, the details of which we learn only in the Epilogue. As Stack prepares to leave for a new posting in Moscow, she receives news that Raheem's son, Mohammed, has been shot dead by US soldiers. Despite this tragedy, Raheem continues to pursue a US visa for himself and his family. Yet when the visa comes through, he holds back. Ironically, it is the financial crisis induced partly by the war, and the withering effect that this has had on the American economy, that persuades him to bide his time in Iraq and see what happens. Raheem is an Iraqi; the freedom he had longed for has come at a terrible price, and he must now ride it out and see where it takes him.

Nora

Key quotes

'Nora had loved America, and she had stood up for it, not so much in words as in deeds. She had embraced the Americans she met, aspired to American-style journalism, travelled to America to be educated.' (p.122)

'I wanted to tell her about rural America, about all the different classes and experiences and geographies she hadn't penetrated when she'd studied in New York ... the America that Nora didn't see, in all its ugly complications and rotting institutions.' (p.122)

'We don't expect anything from the Arab governments. We expect something better from the Americans. That is the *idea* of America.' (p.122)

Stack meets Nora when she first arrives in the Jordanian capital, Amman. An ideal refuge for war-weary reporters, cashed-up refugees and the region's pleasure seekers and playboys, Amman is 'bland ... destined and designed to be passed through on the way to, or from, bigger problems' (p.108). Nora, who picks up Stack 'in a car thick with perfume and pop music' (p.108), embodies the city's shallowness. While Nora travels a similar emotional road to Stack, from innocence to experience, she gains few insights on her journey – hers is a trajectory of loss.

For Nora and her friends, Amman is the perfect place to play at living on the edge. With its security apparatus, the city offers a semblance of threat, but it is a threat that she and her friends are never likely to feel in earnest. They are too deeply embedded in the country's privileges to do anything that would risk their continuing access to them. If Nora affects a sophisticated cynicism about Jordan, she surrenders herself to the myth of America. Educated in the United States, she has somehow retained an unabashed crush on the country and its ideals: 'Nora had loved America, and she had stood up for it, not so much in words as in deeds' (p.122). When news of the torture at Abu Ghraib breaks, she is bereft. Her *idea* of America, her belief that it represents an ideal of hope – somewhere better than the compromised here and the depressing now – is shattered. Without a more robust understanding of the complexities of the country, her image of it cannot survive the first serious setback.

Nora's expectations of the United States are proportionate to her disappointment in her own government, and commensurately unreasonable. She, and many others like her, load their unfulfilled hopes and dreams on the United States and, when it fails to meet their expectations, blame it for their disillusionment. Instead of fixing their problems at home, Nora and those like her seek escape in an impossible dream of US perfection. Her idealism is another version of the hostility that Stack runs into after the invasion of Iraq, when everybody she meets gives their opinions about US foreign policy. The common theme in these diatribes is that, despite its rhetoric, the United States is no better than the dictatorships it condemns. The protestations of disdain are expressions of identification and commonality. Yet America is neither of these things: it is no more the champion of liberty, the home of the free and the land of the brave that Nora imagines, than it is the dead heart of hypocrisy, the calculating human-rights abuser of its enemies' imaginings. Neither entirely good nor entirely evil, it strives to do the right thing and often fails. It is a nuanced country, which Nora, like many others in Jordan, fails to grasp.

Atwar Bahjat

Key quotes

'This is not only the story of Atwar, but the story of Iraq. Her aspirations were the finest hopes of a broken country; her murder reeked of the hopelessness of a lost cause.' (p.195)

'The face on the television screen was etched with the story of her homeland's degeneration. Her skin had grayed, her eyes grown heavy, her face puffed with fatigue. She looked exhausted.' (p.198)

'Atwar looked sick, and so did Iraq. Atwar died, but Iraq just kept bleeding.' (p.198)

If Stack's relationship with Nora dramatises the Arab world's high expectations of and low tolerance for disappointment with the United States, Stack sees in Atwar Bahjat an emblem of the Iraq that might have been but never was. Stack does not have a close relationship with Bahjat: she only meets her once, when she spends a day shadowing her as she works for Al-Jazeera. They cover a routine press conference, and later chat together. Stack promises to keep in touch, but she never does. As such, her relationship to Bahjat is less to do with the Iraqi's memory and more with what she has come to represent.

Stack identifies with Bahjat, admiring the courage she showed in the face of the threats levelled at her. During their day together, they share stories about 'the corrosion of war reporting ... here was a woman my own age, tugged by ambition and emotion, trying to keep intact' (p.193). Bahjat holds a mirror up to Stack – and Stack enjoys the reflection she sees. Just as Bahjat embodies the 'mad hope for an impossible, alternative Iraq: a place of liberated men and women, and the free exchange of ideas; a society that had moved beyond its sectarian differences' (p.195), in the chaos of the insurgency these hopes are as fragile as she is. As her life embodied the hope for a better Iraq, so her death reflects the failure of this hope.

Ahmed

Key quotes

'Even as he spoke I was seeing him as a soul built of black letters on a bright electronic backdrop, a spine and legs and arms constructed of short newspaper paragraphs, representing a generation, representing a sect.' (p.214)

'[He has] the face of a man who is learning, bit by bit, the limitations of empty pockets and lowly family stature.' (p.204)

'I took a chance with their lives ... I came to Iraq in a cloud of violence, part of an American plague. I lured him in with a seductive promise that he was interesting to American readers, that his life had meaning beyond his daily world ... For a young man like Ahmed, shunted aside and mocked, it must have been like a drug. All of that, for a story I never wrote.' (p.216)

Stack makes no bones about the fact that she initially regards Ahmed as little more than a symbol. She had gone 'looking for a young Shiite, somebody whose life and aspirations and circumstances could serve as an emblem for a tortured land' (p.203). In Ahmed, she believes she has found a vehicle for the narrative of contemporary Iraq, an emblem for the experience of a country going to hell. A poor, marginalised Shiite, proud and ambitious, he contains the thwarted energy of a people long held back by the practices of the former regime, and now by the advent of chaos. He is a case study in frustration. They meet and talk regularly, and the story takes shape in Stack's imagination. Yet it doesn't work. Stack cannot confine him within a purely representational framework. In a disturbing, premonitory image, he keeps bleeding beyond the margins of her imposed narrative: 'With Ahmed, I couldn't make it clean ... there I was, sopping at puddles of spilled words, sponging it all onto paper' (p.214).

Ahmed and Stack's meetings are enormously dangerous: an armed guard accompanies Stack to each of them because it has become so perilous to be an American in Iraq. Yet for Ahmed and his girlfriend, Birak, the stakes are even higher. If they are seen associating with an American, there will be 'consequences' (p.215). One day, somebody from one of the militias recognises Birak while she is entering the hotel and promises 'consequences', and this is the last that Stack sees or hears of Birak or Ahmed. She never knows what becomes of them, and is haunted by what may have happened. Stack learns a terrible lesson here: people are not symbols, emblems or metaphors; they are individuals who hope and dream and fear and laugh and cry and bleed and die. It is, in many ways, a discovery that runs counter to her treatment of the other characters throughout her book.

THEMES, IDEAS & VALUES

The uses, abuses and effects of power

Key quotes

'As Americans we have the gift of detaching ourselves and drifting on; it has saved us over and over again from getting mired in guilt or stuck in the past.' (p.3)

'It's about the pain that turns back to gnaw on the tormenter, about the damage we do to others because we want to protect ourselves, and how that damage echoes back into our own souls.' (p.42)

'Really, it is a shame upon us that we have such things.' (p.74)

A key theme of the book is power: its uses, abuses and effects. Stack crosses the region in the wake of invasions and bombings, torture and acts of terror, witnessing their effects. She realises that those who exercise power can suffer as much – in some cases more – damage than their victims. In Israel, she sees the link between small acts of humiliation – the Hasidic boys roughing up the old Palestinian man in East Jerusalem – and the larger exercise of state power, as the Israelis demolish the Palestinian Authority compound in Ramallah. The Israelis' determination to crush the Palestinians has harmed them in ways that their comparatively powerless antagonists have escaped. The Israeli story, Stack reflects, is 'about the pain that turns back to gnaw on the tormenter, about the damage we do to others because we want to protect ourselves, and how that damage echoes back into our own souls' (p.42). That damage in Israel, Stack argues, is reflected in a moral failure, in the victors' inability to recognise the humanity of their vanquished cohabiters.

Miri, the liberal photographer, believes that Palestinian children can be taught to stop torturing animals by being encouraged to think of them as akin to people, with personalities and feelings. While she is explaining this to Stack, the two are watching a news item about a talent show in a 'jolly and clean' Israeli prison (p.45). When Stack observes, 'That's not where they put the Palestinians', Miri responds: 'No ... That's for regular prisoners. Criminals. Not the Palestinians' (p.45). Miri, good-hearted and committed to the peace process, seemingly cannot recognise the contradiction between her compassion for animals and her acceptance of the treatment of the Palestinian prisoners. This reflects how each side in the conflict has lost an essential empathy, and as a result is confined to its own intellectual prison. To believe in one's humanity, as each side does in this case, is to be blind to one's capacity for brutality; yet to repudiate one's capacity for both is to deny one's humanity. For Stack, the Israelis' behaviour is of especial interest, as it furnishes a model for America's emerging military and moral trajectory. As America exercises ever-greater levels of violence in pursuit of peace and security, it must not, Stack cautions, lose touch with its inner moral compass.

Stack also spends time interviewing men and women who have suffered under tyranny. She meets those who can't stop talking about what happened to them, those too deeply ashamed to admit what they have suffered and those who can tell nobody for fear of further mistreatment. The whole region is awash with perpetrators and their victims: 'The Middle East was divided into three classes: the torturers, the tortured, and those who stayed out of the way' (p.120). Where a political system rests on fear and humiliation, it damages those who wield power as much as it distorts those who are subject to it. After an Iraqi merchant in Najaf recalled his own experience of torture – his fingernails were pulled out; he was hung from a ceiling, electrified and had dogs set upon him – he confides to Stack, 'Really, it is a shame upon us that we have such things' (p.74). At last, she reflects, 'somebody had finally said it out loud', spoken the great unspoken truth of the region and its people:

> These people were embarrassed about what they had endured, about the parts they had been forced to play – victims or tormentors, it was all unendurably shameful. They had been

> co-opted, tortured, spied upon, and had spied themselves. They had sunk deeper and deeper into collective guilt ... They felt inferior, as if something must be wrong with themselves, in their culture or their souls. (p.74)

Feeling this way, convinced of their own moral and spiritual infirmity, they objectify their anger and shame by heaping humiliations on their political opponents, their ethnic enemies, their neighbours – guilty and innocent alike. And so the cycle of abuse renews itself, and the region and its governments stagger from one abusive regime to another.

Key point

Power, if used unjustly or disproportionately, dehumanises both its victims and its agents.

Representation and its challenges

Key quotes

'In Afghanistan, I kept waiting for a narrative to assert itself.' (p.27)

'The invasion was a nasty, impersonal force, and people had been walloped. And me, pretending I could encapsulate it all in a few paragraphs, grabbing a quote from this victim or that, scribbling scraps of description.' (p.60)

As a journalist, Stack's principal responsibility is to make sense of the events she witnesses and to render to her readers an authoritative, informed and readable account of these events and the broader context in which they fit. It is a responsibility she more than acquits. She is a gifted and dedicated reporter prepared to risk all for a good story. Yet she is regularly forced to reflect on the difficulties or, in some cases, futility of her task. While reporting on the hunt for Osama bin Laden in the Tora Bora cave complex, she is struck by the problem of imposing recognisable form on an operation that is so chaotic:

> News writers depend upon the world to organize itself into some kind of tale, a story that can be told in short, recognizable form. People rise and fall; murder and redeem; cheat and reconcile. In Afghanistan, I kept waiting for a narrative to assert itself. (p.27)

The war on terror is being fought in the thin air of the mountains by half-starved mujahideen, some of them bin Laden's former allies, where it is uncertain who is friend, who is foe, and indeed whether any fighting is actually taking place. Stack realises that no recognisable form will present itself, and that any account of these events that makes it look like a conventional 'battle' will be a falsehood: '[E]vents flickered, split, and rolled away like mercury. To write about the battle in an organized way, to shuffle the pieces, tap the sides, and square it into paragraphs and quotations was a fabrication' (p.28). Stack is caught in a difficult position. As a reporter covering the war on terror, she is tasked with offering an honest and reliable representation of societies wrestling with chaos, but her account must also be accessible to her readers. As such, she has to offer a clear, ordered and sequential representation of places and events that are entirely devoid of such qualities. She must strike a balance between her roles as witness and interpreter. It is no small challenge.

On other occasions, Stack is overwhelmed by the responsibility she bears and conscious of the inadequacy of the tools at her disposal. Seeing the bodies piled up in a makeshift morgue at a Baghdad children's hospital, with more arriving by the hour, she is suddenly struck by the fact that she is a witness to the collapse of a once sophisticated society. Where the US domestic media has a neat storyline to slip over these events, Stack is confronted by the untidy reality that no simple narrative can hope to capture or convey, and she despairs of her task:

> The story line of the news reports – a dictator toppled; the hunt for weapons of mass destruction; the officials in Washington wearing suits and uniforms and congratulating themselves on Operation Enduring Freedom – what did any of that have to do with the waste of these families, trawling

> in the chaos for one particular person? The invasion was a nasty, impersonal force, and people had been walloped. And me, pretending I could encapsulate it all in a few paragraphs, grabbing a quote from this victim or that, scribbling scraps of description. (p.60)

Stack is engaged in a constant battle to find narrative strategies that enable her to do justice to the people whose suffering she witnesses and to tell the complex stories of the societies and regions from which they come. It is in this context that she makes such frequent use of symbolic figures, creating metaphors out of the people she encounters, using them to carry the story of their country and its travails.

There are a number of examples of this – Mohammed Zaman, Ahmed, Nora – but another symbol is Stack herself. She identifies at the book's outset as 'extremely American' (p.3), and in many ways her journey through the book traces America's journey through the war on terror. As she struggles to understand the region and its challenges, so the noble purpose America carried into Afghanistan is dissipated and lost. As she struggles to keep the blood off her shoes in Iraq, so the nation steeps itself further in slaughter, and nothing can keep its mark off her. Enraged by Saudi Arabia's appalling gender inequities, Stack confronts the compromises that US dependence on Saudi oil imposes on America's espoused values. Meanwhile the Israel–Palestine conflict festers on, stoking the fires of hatred and drawing America ever deeper into the quagmire of the region. The costs of this engagement are measured in dollars, soldiers' lives and damaged credibility, all of which are channelled through Stack's psychological fragmentation, moral examination and deepening disillusionment.

Key point

Stack consistently regards the war as a set of descriptive problems, asking herself how she can best convey or describe an event or a moment. But her development, as both a writer and a person, is marked by her increasing recognition of the human dimension of the tragedies she describes.

Black, white and grey

Key quotes

'If he's telling the truth, he's lying. If he's lying, he's telling the truth. That was Afghanistan after September 11.' (p.9)

'War cannot be innocent, but sometimes it is naive. At first the fight in Afghanistan felt finite and comprehensible. There had been an attack, an act of war, and America responded with conventional warfare against an objectively violent and repressive regime … there was an internal logic, the suggestion of a moral thread, of cause and effect. And so we plunged forward, and our eyes were bound in gauze.' (pp.13–14)

'American officials talked about "the enemy" and "the evildoers" and it sounded odd, empty, like a legend. Even in the heights of Tora Bora, on the front lines of this vague new war, the enemy was nowhere to be seen. He was just a rumor, secreted in shadows.' (p.28)

In a political and military context as fraught as the Middle East – with its ancient enmities of religion and tribe, the powerful and the powerless, the torturers and the defenders of human rights – it is tempting to think about the region and its conflicts in terms of black and white. But this is to misunderstand the complex affinities that underlie these questions of life and death, and thereby to miss the undertones beneath the overt politics of self-justification. Stack gets her first inkling that there's more to these conflicts than the simple script of good versus evil on her first assignment in Afghanistan. Primed by America's wounded rhetoric – Bush's famous comment, 'Either you are with us or you are with the terrorists' – Stack arrives in Afghanistan expecting a straightforward battle between friend and foe. But no such struggle occurs. Stuck up in the mountains near Tora Bora, Stack reflects that the language of 'the enemy' and 'the evildoers' sounded 'odd, empty, like a legend' because 'the enemy was nowhere to be seen' (p.28).

If up in the mountains the enemy is conspicuous by his absence, down in the plains it seems he is everywhere. When Zaman's arch-enemy, Hazrat Ali, arrives in Jalalabad and is appointed local security chief, a reporter asks him: 'Where are the Taliban?' His response is a surprise: 'What do you mean? They're in their offices' (p.18). The Taliban may have been defeated, but that doesn't mean they've lost power. Their functionaries fill the bureaucracy, and the only way for the new administration to operate is to work with them. As one of Stack's Afghan friends tells her: 'The Taliban was 95 percent of our country ... Look around you. We didn't kill everybody' (p.19).

Hence, the straightforward moral crusade that the Americans expected in Afghanistan, and the task that embodied this – the capture of Osama bin Laden – never eventuated. They ran headlong into the dizzying tangle of Afghan political, familial and tribal alliances. The Americans never recovered their sense of purpose: 'Catching bin Laden was the first important thing the United States set out to do after September 11. The job was bungled so thoroughly that the war never really found its compass again' (p.10). Though the simple equation that fired Americans' righteous anger – the belief that you are either for us or against us – may have provided a form of moral comfort, it ill-equipped them for the task at hand and crippled their capacity to operate effectively across the region.

It is in Israel that Stack confronts the true complexity of the region. Here, Israelis and Palestinians, 'locked in a death match for survival', justify their actions by believing the best about themselves and the worst about the other:

> Israel is merciful; Israel is brutal. The two deathless storylines of the Jewish state ... Most people believe one or the other, and believe it fervently. It is hard to find anybody who acknowledges that both might be true, and then some. (p.41)

Yet in this context the simple polarity of good and evil is less an objective fact than a matter of political or religious commitment. Indeed, as Stack points out, the antagonists are opposites in the same way that two sides of a coin are opposed, as the indivisible parts of a single entity:

> Israelis and Palestinians had become what they never wished to be – one people after all, each one half of a whole, locked together in a union you could not touch or understand from the outside. (p.41)

To come blundering into these complex relationships armed only with the certainty of one's moral righteousness, as the United States does – dividing the world into those for and against them, indifferent to the deeply textured history of the places they enter – is to visit misery on the inhabitants and guarantee the failure of the mission. Sometimes, as the Americans discover in Afghanistan and Iraq, brute force is not enough to get you what you want.

Oppression of women

Key quotes

'As if the freedom of these women, caught in the strings of their marriages, family honor, tribal code, and morality police, could come so cheap.' (p.20)

'In the end, you can't lose yourself. You can drape your body in black, you can smother your breasts and cover your face and drown yourself in expensive perfumes until your smells, too, are submerged ... but you will still be a woman ... You can hide but you can't disappear.' (p.138)

In a region racked by headline-grabbing conflicts, Stack gains a unique insight into the most widespread but hidden form of violence and oppression: the treatment of women. Where men fight and die in wars, are targeted by death squads, or are kidnapped or tortured, the violence against women is so institutionalised, so much a feature of the cultural landscape of the region, that it is virtually invisible – especially to male reporters. This is the hidden oppression in a region preoccupied with more 'newsworthy' forms of political or military subjugation – it is the nine-tenths of the iceberg of oppression that lurks below the surface. Half of the people in the region are treated as second-class citizens, and hardly anyone regards this as a matter of note.

As a woman, Stack is granted privileged access to this hidden world, with its silent resentments and private palliations (comforts), its thwarted dreams and its adamantine (unyielding) defiance. In Jalalabad, she visits the home of her translator, Naseer, where she spends time with his female relatives, 'spectacular women, their cheeks and eyes full of light' (p.19). They inhabit a world infinitely removed from the life Stack leads, immured from its demands and possibilities. Stack observes that their 'tiny universe – tight rooms with dirt floors strung around a muddy courtyard' feels 'sealed off' from Jalalabad, and that '[t]his was only the first layer of withdrawal: Jalalabad was far removed from Kabul, and Kabul from the rest of the world' (p.20). In America, it is believed that these women have been 'liberated' by the removal of the Taliban. In fact, the change of government has altered nothing in these women's lives.

Nevertheless, although they may be prisoners of their culture, they are not victims. Stack marvels at their vitality and boldness. When Naseer's wife, Sediqa, gives birth to a daughter, the women celebrate with music and dancing: 'The women were stomping and arching, shaking their hips ... It was sexy, sultry, joyful. They were dancing for a new life, another soul indoctrinated into their private sorority' (p.21). They may be walled in, hidden by headscarves and veils, but these women are defiant. Just as no foreign government can grant them liberty, so their own cannot rob them of their essential spirit.

In Saudi Arabia, the situation is even more bleak. Of all the places from which Stack reports, this is the one she finds most challenging. When she is being bombed by the Israeli air force or threatened by Iraqi gunmen, there is a quality of impersonality about these threats: it isn't personal; she is just in the wrong place at the wrong time. Yet in Saudi Arabia, the assault could not be more personal. She is treated as a second-class citizen not because of what she *does* but because of what she *is*. The authoritarian politics of the monarchy trickle down through the society, as those who have power abuse and humiliate those who do not. At the bottom of this chain of misery sit women and children. Without rights or protections, they are at the mercy of men, who, provided they avoid political provocation, are free to act as they will. Hence the tales of child and spousal abuse that the law can punish, in a limited fashion, but whose victims can be afforded no protection.

When Stack is on the receiving end of the mildest forms of this discrimination in Saudi Arabia – ejected from the men-only area at Starbucks and asked to move away from the door of the bank so as not to 'provoke' the men within – she is furious, but feels impotent. Her government, bound by laws and regulations regarding equal opportunity, equal access to services and equal treatment before the law regardless of gender, is happy to look the other way in Saudi Arabia, seduced by the lure of oil and its obscene profits. Worse, Stack is compelled to confront her own complicity with this appalling regime. If the US government has turned its back on Saudi Arabia's women for oil, Stack is prepared to share in their humiliations because, like the government and the oil companies, she stands to gain something – access and stories. If what she is offends the Saudis, then Stack can at least take refuge in what she does. There can be no such escape for the vast majority of the country's women.

Surviving and not surviving

Key quotes

'[T]he wars are still happening, and they have been happening all along. People died. Promises were broken. Things were destroyed. And as Americans these actions belong to us. We should remember those days, or we should admit they meant nothing, and if they meant nothing then there is the question of how much we have lost, and why.' (pp.3–4)

'You can be anywhere if you're not really there. You can walk into any room, drive down any road, ask any question, write about anybody's pain. You tell yourself you are unscathed … It occurs to me now that maybe this is the most American trait of all, the trademark of these wars. To be there and be gone all at once, to tell ourselves it just happened, we did what we did but we had no control over the consequences.' (p.240)

'But we lived through it, and we are living still. And in the end, survival is not a meager redemption; it is substantial and it will not last forever, either.' (p.251)

Stack's experiences are bookended by her recognition that, just as she had intuited from the story of her father's cousin, 'You can survive and not survive, both at the same time' (p.4). The book consistently returns to the question of survival: what does it mean to survive, and how, in the chaos of conflict or the dark night of tyranny, can one hope to do so? The question can only be answered by considering two other, related questions. What is life and what is death? How might one live, and how should one die?

Stack's journeys through the war on terror bring her into contact, at one point or another, with an improbable set of characters: despots and warlords, apologists and opponents, fighters and refugees, survivors and damaged individuals. What these encounters demonstrate to Stack is that there's a good deal more to survival than a functioning heartbeat; you can live but you might be dead in every other respect. Just as those who oppress their fellow citizens have surrendered their humanity to the regime they serve, so those they terrorise into silence, or torture and abuse, lose an essential part of themselves, a basic self-respect without which they can scarcely tolerate themselves. These people are alive, but the better, human part of them has died.

Likewise, Stack meets those who seem to have lost everything that makes them human: they have suffered terrible indignities; seen their loved ones abused, abducted or killed; lost their homes, their livelihoods, their minds; and been reduced to half-demented beggars shaking their fists at the sky in impotent fury. But as long as they bear witness to the injustice they suffer, as long as they affirm the truth of what has happened to them, though these people may die, they and the causes they serve will live on.

To live, Stack realises, you must hold onto, or recover, some essential inner dignity, retain faith with a moral or philosophical code external to the self or a more imperative inner truth. You must keep some part of the self inviolable. To do this, you must live *for* something

– a political cause, faith, a professional calling, love. Then, whatever the blows suffered or the scars borne, you will still hold onto that thing that gives life purpose. You may not live, but you'll survive.

DIFFERENT INTERPRETATIONS

Different interpretations arise from different responses to a text. Over time, a text will give rise to a wide range of responses from its readers, who may come from various social or cultural groups and live in very different places and historical periods. Responses by critics and reviewers can be published in newspapers, journals and books, both online and in print. They can also be expressed in discussions among readers in the media, classrooms, book groups and so on.

While there is no single correct reading or interpretation of a text, it is important to understand that an interpretation is more than a personal opinion – it is the justification of a point of view on the text. To present an interpretation of a text based on your point of view you must use a logical argument and support it with relevant evidence from the text.

Critical viewpoints

Every Man in This Village Is a Liar was published in 2010 and was widely reviewed at the time – primarily in the United States and the United Kingdom, and to a lesser extent in Australia. The following discussion draws on a range of reviews that appeared in the print media.

Notably, most reviewers regard the book as being focused primarily on Stack and her experiences. She is praised for the honesty of her account, her refusal to pretend that she knew more about what she saw or what was happening than she did. In *The Independent*, Adrian Hamilton notes, '[W]hat makes this such a refreshing, and revealing book is that Stack never makes herself into anything other than she is, a woman, an American, young, naive and even innocent.' She is likewise lauded for her acuity – her capacity to zero in on the telling detail and to render a scene with brevity and clarity: Kamila Shamsie, writing in *The Guardian*, comments, 'In a single sentence she can conjure up mood and atmosphere.'

Above all, the book is praised for its compassion, for its readiness to look behind the statistics and the large-scale political picture, and not merely to notice but also to evoke, and to write with feeling, about how the lives of ordinary people have been distorted by dictatorship and crippled by war. Accordingly, while Stack is commended for her journalistic prowess, a number of the reviews reflect on the fact that the book's particular value arises from those parts of it where Stack abandons her professional objectivity. She is at her best, the reviewers concur, when she stops detaching herself from what she witnesses and immerses herself in it; when she stops being a war reporter and experiences events directly.

The work has also been praised for its engagement with the politics of the war on terror, its origins and consequences. Some reviewers prized the insights it offers into the sources of terror in the societies Stack covers, the role of US policy in alleviating or exacerbating local conditions, and the moral and policy quandaries raised by America's alliances with the region's tyrants and dictators. Marla Stone, in the *Los Angeles Times*, notes, 'For Stack, the violence that distorts life in the Middle East is the explosive product of sectarian division, authoritarian local governments and self-serving and short-sighted American policy.' Several reviews included reference to Stack's assertion that the war on terror never existed, proposing that the book is more sensational than it actually is. Yet at least one review recognised that the book was more iconoclastic (attacking conventional beliefs or ideas) than sensational, more analytical than attention-seeking.

As such, while critical opinion on the book has generally been favourable, there is a notable divide between those who regard the book as being essentially a species of autobiography and those who regard it as a more politically engaged text, focusing on the damage done by US intervention in an already fragile part of the world.

Two interpretations

Drawing on this division in the book's critical reception, the following outlines two different interpretations: one that approaches the text as a work of autobiography, focused on the personal and psychological changes that the war wrought on Stack; and one that sees it as a more overtly analytical book, engaged with the political and moral questions raised by the war on terror.

Interpretation 1: *Every Man in This Village Is a Liar* is a powerful personal account of the experience of covering war, and its effects on the reporter.

How refreshing to read a book about the war on terror that is not overburdened with the complex backstory of age-old regional conflicts. The weight of history lies heavy in the Middle East, and there are more than enough analyses out there of who did what to whom, when, what they did in return and where this has left them now. Here is a book that offers a fresh perspective on an old story thanks to a bravura performance from a first-time writer who knows what she knows and makes no effort to pretend to knowledge that she doesn't have.

Megan Stack was the *Los Angeles Times'* Houston bureau chief when the September 11 attacks found her on holiday in Paris. Closer to where the action was about to take place, and unencumbered by the travel restrictions that kept her more experienced colleagues grounded in the United States, she was sent to Afghanistan to watch the Americans take their revenge against the government that had sheltered Osama bin Laden. Stack is open about the fact that she has little idea of what she is doing at first. She is in love with the idea of being a foreign correspondent, but has nothing to guide her in her new career beyond the nose for a good story, tenacity and great courage.

At first Stack seems quite fearless in the face of death – indeed, worryingly so. Unmoved by news of the murder of colleagues, she frets that her response is abnormal: 'I know that I should feel something; to feel something is appropriate and human' (p.8). Though she doubts her humanity, the cause of her numbness is not the proximity of death but its unreality. So thoroughly grounded in the certainties of the world she has recently left, she cannot yet conceive of death as a real presence. It is not long before she revises this view, and her responses to the death and destruction she witnesses, and the damaged people she encounters, across the Middle East, the Arabian Peninsula and North Africa demonstrates that, if anything, her problem is not a lack of humanity but an excess of it.

As a reporter, Stack's job is to take her readers with her into strange and often unsettling places, to familiarise them with the contours of what is happening and who is affected by it, and also, perhaps more importantly, to convey something of the flavour of a place. Her prose is ideal for this task; it fixes on the telling details that bring a place or a person to life:

> I was carried along by anxious bodies, through marble hallways and reception rooms as big as bowling alleys, laid with Persian carpets and cornered with Phoenician artifacts ... Waiters circled with thimbles of bitter yellow coffee and teacups fragile as skin. (p.160)

As the book progresses, Stack focuses on the victims of the war on terror. While the political class jostle for power and enjoy its fruits or take their defeats as they come, it is the ordinary citizens who increasingly attract Stack's attention. They are denied jobs by political prejudice, tortured for speaking out against oppression, terrorised because they belong to the wrong religious sect, blown up while queuing for a job, shot for associating with the wrong people, bombed out of their homes and reduced to humiliating indigence (lacking the essentials of life). Stack evokes their sufferings with sensitivity and real anger. She is moved by the plight of these people, and she makes no pretence of journalistic objectivity when describing their lot.

Perhaps she feels their pain so acutely because, in the final chapters of the book, she comes to share it. Covering Israel's bombardment of southern Lebanon, Stack finds that, like the cowering or fleeing civilians she meets there, she is regarded as a legitimate target. She discovers what it is to live in terror:

> A few days under bombardment teach you everything about your nerves ... how they can vibrate and ache and make you

> shake, make you want to bite right through your finger or peel your skin off your body just to get free of them. (p.224)

Her experience of war has brought her to the realisation that she has survived for so long only by emotionally absenting herself from the terrible things she has witnessed. Stack acknowledges that she got 'tougher and smaller' and pulled back 'behind my face, behind the interviews, behind the stories': '[T]he harder it got, the more I drew myself in, the more I distracted myself with colourful myths ... That works fine until all of a sudden it doesn't work at all' (p.240). Older, wiser about the moral compromises to which the war on terror has led the United States, disillusioned but physically whole, Stack realises that though she has survived the war, she has also not survived it. The country she knew has changed, and she too has been irrevocably altered by her experiences. She will never find her way back to the person that she was. Nothing will ever be the same.

Interpretation 2: *Every Man in This Village Is a Liar* offers a sophisticated insight into the moral and political landscape of the war on terror.

Megan Stack's *Every Man in This Village Is a Liar* is far more than one reporter's dispatches from life on the front line. Her presentation of herself as a naive reporter thrown in at the deep end as a foreign correspondent belies the sophistication of the book's analysis of the moral and political landscape carved out by the war on terror. Yet just as Stack is no ingenue, so she's no political scientist. She is instead an open-eyed observer, unencumbered by – or progressively divested of – political illusions and blind patriotism, ready to tell the uncomfortable truths about the broken societies she travels through, and the damage wrought on them by US intervention.

Stack is able to tell this story so well because she brings a fresh and unprejudiced eye to the entrenched animosities of the region. She has no investment in protecting the interests of one side or the other, and calls out ignorance and abuse whether she finds it in Baghdad, Beirut, Jerusalem or Tripoli. While she is clear-eyed about the damage that

US intervention has done to these countries – visiting chaos on some and further entrenching dictatorship in others – she recognises that the violence here has deeper roots. Stack is unflinching in her examination of the sectarian divisions that scar the region: she considers the long-term harm done to individuals and societies by unaccountable and brutal governments, measuring both in the disrupted or curtailed lives of individuals whose worst sin, often, is the misfortune to have been born in the wrong place at the wrong time. She is gifted with an eye for the telling details that bring to life the destruction wrought on these people. In the bombed village of Bint Jbeil, its buildings 'crushed and crumbled into great dunes of wreckage' (p.232), she sees the archaeology of once ordinary lives laid bare: 'The blasted fixtures of a chandelier shop poke at crooked angles. Somebody's lingerie drawer hangs open, bras dripping down like vines' (p.234).

Yet Stack's work is at its strongest when she interrogates the moral and political price of the war on terror for America – where its alliances with the region's dictators have taken it. She maps a landscape of compromise and complicity that, in the longer term, may leave the United States in a weaker position. The country's cynical abandonment of its animating principles – the promotion of democracy and the defence of human rights – in pursuit of its immediate enemies not only leave it open to justifiable charges of hypocrisy but also corrode the citizens' trust that it has so slowly been able to build. The most notable casualty of the war on terror, Stack proposes, might be America itself.

One of the book's most important aspects is its focus on women: its linking of casual discrimination, in societies that routinely regard women as second-class citizens or chattels, with broader patterns of political oppression that the war on terror has ultimately served to entrench. Stack writes about these matters with feeling because, as a woman in Afghanistan, Yemen and Saudi Arabia, she experiences them directly. Driven out of the men-only section of Starbucks, she is sent to the 'family' section:

> As a woman, that's where I belong. I have no right to mix with male customers or sit in view of passing shoppers. I must confine myself to the separate, inferior, and usually invisible spaces where Saudi Arabia shunts half the population. (p.129)

War takes its toll on Stack, and she ends the book in a perilous psychological state. But, while she is grateful for having survived, it is the lives of the innocent thousands, destroyed by careless US intervention into already volatile political environments, that live on in the reader's memory.

QUESTIONS & ANSWERS

This section focuses on your own analytical writing on the text, and gives you strategies for producing high-quality responses in your coursework and exam essays.

Essay writing – an overview

An essay on a literary work is a formal and serious piece of writing that presents your point of view on the text, usually in response to a given topic. Your 'point of view' in an essay is your interpretation of the meaning of the text's language, structure, characters, situations and events, supported by detailed analysis of textual evidence.

Analyse – don't summarise

In your essays it is important to avoid simply summarising what happens in a text.

- A summary is a description or paraphrase (retelling in different words) of the characters and events. For example: 'Macbeth has a horrifying vision of a dagger dripping with blood before he goes to murder King Duncan.'
- An analysis is an explanation of the real meaning or significance that lies 'beneath' the text's words (and images, for a film). For example: 'Macbeth's vision of a bloody dagger shows how deeply uneasy he is about the violent act he is contemplating – as well as his sense that supernatural forces are impelling him to act.'

A limited amount of summary is sometimes necessary to let your reader know which part of the text you wish to discuss. However, always keep this to a minimum and follow it immediately with your analysis of what this part of the text is really telling us.

Plan your essay

Carefully plan your essay so that you have a clear idea of what you are going to say. The plan ensures that your ideas flow logically, that your argument remains consistent and that you stay on the topic. An essay plan should be a list of brief dot points – no more than half a page.

- Include your central argument or main contention – a concise statement (usually in a single sentence) of your overall response to the topic. See 'Analysing a sample topic' for guidelines on how to formulate a main contention.
- Write three or four dot points for each paragraph indicating the main idea and evidence/examples from the text. Note that in your essay you will need to *expand* on these points and *analyse* the evidence.

Structure your essay

An essay is a complete, self-contained piece of writing. It has a clear beginning (the introduction), middle (several body paragraphs) and end (the last paragraph or conclusion). It must also have a central argument that runs throughout, linking each paragraph to form a coherent whole. See examples of introductions and conclusions in the 'Analysing a sample topic' and 'Sample answer' sections.

The introduction establishes your overall response to the topic. It includes your main contention and outlines the main evidence you will refer to in the course of the essay. Write your introduction *after* you have done a plan and *before* you write the rest of the essay.

The body paragraphs argue your case – they present evidence from the text and explain how this evidence supports your argument. Each body paragraph needs:

- a strong **topic sentence** (usually the first sentence) that states the main point being made in the paragraph
- **evidence** from the text, including some brief quotations
- **analysis** of the textual evidence, explaining its significance, and **explanation** of how it supports your argument
- **links back to the topic** in one or more statements, usually towards the end of the paragraph.

Connect the body paragraphs so that your discussion flows smoothly. Use some linking words and phrases such as 'similarly' and 'on the other hand', though don't start every paragraph like this. Another strategy is to use a significant word from the last sentence of one paragraph in the first sentence of the next.

Use key terms from the topic – or synonyms for them – throughout, so the relevance of your discussion to the topic is always clear.

The conclusion ties everything together and finishes the essay. It includes strong statements that emphasise your central argument and provide a clear response to the topic.

Avoid simply restating the points made earlier in the essay – this will end on a very flat note and imply that you have run out of ideas and vocabulary. The conclusion is meant to be a logical extension of what you have written, not just a repetition or summary of it. Writing an effective conclusion can be a challenge. Try using these tips:

- Start by linking back to the final sentence of the second-last paragraph – this helps your writing to 'flow', rather than leaping back to your main contention straight away.
- Use synonyms and expressions with equivalent meanings to vary your vocabulary. This allows you to reinforce your line of argument without being repetitive.
- When planning your essay, think of one or two broad statements or observations about the text's wider meaning. These should be related to the topic and your overall argument. Keep them for the conclusion, since they will give you something 'new' to say but still follow logically from your discussion. The introduction will be focused on the topic, but the conclusion can present a wider view of the text.

Essay topics

1 How does Stack employ symbolic figures to make the complex story of the war on terror more accessible to her readers?

2 "You can survive and not survive, both at the same time." In what senses does Stack 'survive and not survive' her experiences?

3 How does the title of Stack's book hint at its deeper themes of truth, falsehood, certainty and indeterminacy?

4 What does Stack's treatment of Ahmed reveal to her about the nature and responsibilities of her profession?

5 Is Nora's dismay about the revelations from Abu Ghraib an expression of naivety, or does it reveal something deeper about America's role and status in the Middle East?

6 One of America's main aims in the war on terror is to make the United States and its people feel secure. On the basis of the evidence that Stack presents, has the project been a success?

7 Explore Atwar Bahjat's role as an emblem of Iraqi hope and the dashing of those hopes.

8 'We perceive events in the book from Stack's perspective; this makes it impossible to view events from the perspective of the people she describes.' Discuss.

9 "Back then the future looked clean and good, and Raheem was full of simple hope ... I've never seen him so happy again." How does Raheem's story reflect the experience of modern Iraq?

10 Discuss the representations of women in the text. How are women viewed in Afghanistan, Iraq and Saudi Arabia, and how does this differ from how they are viewed in America?

Vocabulary for writing on *Every Man in This Village Is a Liar*

Bildungsroman: a text (usually a novel) that traces the formation or youthful development of the protagonist and the process by which they attain maturity.

Burqa: a long, loose garment worn by some Islamic women to cover their bodies from head to feet when they are in public.

Metaphor: a figure of speech in which one thing is described in terms of another.

Mujahideen: means 'those who struggle'; refers to warriors fighting a holy war.

Symbol: an object or a person who stands for something else.

Thobe: a long-sleeved tunic, or shirt-like garment, that reaches from the neck to the ankle. It is a common form of dress among Islamic males throughout the Arabian Peninsula and the Middle East, and is sometimes known as a *dishdasha*.

Analysing a sample topic

"You can survive and not survive, both at the same time." In what senses does Stack 'survive and not survive' her experiences?

This topic asks you to explore the notion of physical and psychological survival in the aftermath of conflict. It invites you to examine the ways in which the experience of reporting on war affected and ultimately changed Stack.

The topic includes a quotation from the text, and it is important to understand the context of the quotation in order to respond to the topic question. This statement appears in the prologue, in which Stack reflects on what she has learned from her experiences. Stack claims this idea that 'you can survive and not survive' was the first lesson she learned about war, due to a relative's suicide after his experiences in Beirut. This indicates, through a tragic story, that the psychological effects of war can be as great, or greater than, the immediate physical effects.

A prompt such as this invites you to think carefully about the idea of survival. Some questions to consider include:

- What constitutes survival? Can it be more than merely physical?
- Can the mental effects of war leave traces long after the physical effects have disappeared?
- Will someone working in a war zone, witnessing terrible events, always carry the marks of this experience with them?
- Is a witness to events also a survivor of them?
- Is survival an ongoing process?

It may also help to look up 'survival' in a dictionary, or brainstorm ideas about different types of survival, in order to develop your own understanding of the term and explore a range of ideas surrounding it.

Below is a brief outline of how you might approach this topic.

Sample introduction

> Megan Stack is both a survivor and a victim of the war on terror. She prefaces her book with the assertion, 'You can survive and not survive, both at the same time'; as the narrative progresses, we come to understand the truth of her statement. Stack survives her experiences physically; yet in another sense she does not survive the war, as she bears the emotional scars of what she has witnessed. At the end of the book we see her war-weary and struggling to function. We see, too, that Stack undertakes a journey from innocence to experience; in some ways, the person she was does not survive, but a wiser individual, with a more complex sense of allegiance to her country, emerges.

Body paragraph outline

Paragraph 1: Stack survives physically, although her survival is accompanied by guilt that others did not.

- Stack survives her meetings with Ahmed, although she never finds out if he does, and she feels guilty that she exposed him to danger.
- She survives the Israeli bombardment in Lebanon. This is the first time she has felt like a 'target', leading her to understand the suffering that others experience daily.
- She leaves the Middle East, but Raheem and his son do not, causing us to reflect on their relative positions: Stack is an American journalist able to leave with comparative ease; Raheem and his family are Iraqis trying to survive the war.

Paragraph 2: While Stack leaves the Middle East without physical injury, she bears the emotional scars of her experience.

- Stack begins to break down after experiencing the Israeli bombing of southern Lebanon, realising that she has suffered psychologically.

- She feels immense guilt over seeking out Ahmed, putting him in danger and possibly bringing about his death.
- As an American citizen, she feels guilt over and responsibility for what she comes to see as a mistaken intervention by a reckless government.

Paragraph 3: Stack's naivety and innocence do not survive the war, but she gains experience and wisdom.

- Much like the United States, Stack compromises her morals and values as the war progresses. In Saudi Arabia, she complies with the country's discrimination against women in order to gain access to sources for stories.
- She puts Ahmed in danger, though she doesn't realise how badly until he disappears; she learns quickly that the regimes she is reporting on are far more dangerous for their citizens than for her.
- Stack begins the book as 'very American', but as she sees the effects of the war on terror she begins to question both the war and her once simple allegiance to America.

Sample conclusion

> *Every Man in This Village Is a Liar* shows various ways in which Stack both survives and does not survive. Her experiences in the Middle East leave her scarred emotionally, but also give her new insight. From this, we see that survival is not a simple matter of living or dying, but rather a complex, ongoing process of experiencing the present and making peace with the past. In framing her experience in terms of survival, Stack invites us to question the true costs of the war on terror, and to count among its victims not only the dead but also the emotionally wounded – and among these, Stack herself.

SAMPLE ANSWER

What does Stack's treatment of Ahmed reveal to her about the nature and responsibilities of her profession?

Every Man in This Village Is a Liar examines Megan Stack's journey from innocence to experience, both personally and professionally. Her relationship with Ahmed is integral to this journey, as through Ahmed, Stack sees that journalism requires using others' stories to communicate effectively. She also learns that journalists have a great responsibility to protect their sources; the desire for truth should be tempered with respect for human life. Finally, she gains a heightened appreciation of the reporter's responsibility to represent people fairly: to look beyond symbols and rhetoric to do justice to the individual.

Stack comes to realise that journalism is not only about finding information, but also about communicating it in a way that will resonate. Stack enters the war a naive young reporter, 'very American', supportive of the United States' search for bin Laden. From the beginning, she is conscious of the need to trace the story of the war – to find 'a narrative' – but she struggles to do so. Afghanistan is a surge of distractions – 'meaning washed away in floods of colour' – and it is never clear whom to trust: 'If he's telling the truth, he's lying. If he's lying, he's telling the truth.' Stack begins to realise that this war will require more than simple reportage and traditional journalistic techniques; it will require a more complex mode of interacting with sources and reporting on events.

By the time Stack enters Iraq in 2006, she has developed journalistic techniques to report on the war effectively. In particular, Stack often uses an individual or group to stand for a population: we see this with the 'living martyr', who is used to represent all Shiites, and with the American women on the oil compound, who are used to characterise American families in Saudi Arabia. In Iraq, she sets out to find an individual with the express purpose of using him symbolically: 'I went looking for a young Shiite ... [who] could serve as an emblem for a tortured land.' Initially Stack does not realise the effect of this, but as she comes to know Ahmed, she reflects that her desire to make him into a symbol reveals something about the nature of journalism. Reporting involves both truth-telling and distortion; in the selection of individuals to represent many others, it constructs a version of reality to suit its own ends: 'Even as he spoke I was seeing him as a soul built of black letters ... a spine and arms and legs constructed of short newspaper paragraphs.'

Stack knows that her meetings with Ahmed are hazardous: she details the precautions they take and reflects during their first interview, 'Everybody is getting killed these days.' But she still encourages him to meet several times, luring him 'with the seductive promise that he was interesting to American readers'. While Stack has a guard to protect her on forays out of the office, Ahmed and his girlfriend, Birak, have no-one to accompany them.

When Birak is recognised and 'consequences' are promised, Stack is aware of the significance: 'I sit perfectly still, frozen, understanding.' Yet only when it is clear that she will not hear from Ahmed again does she realise she has not truly appreciated the danger, confessing, 'I took a chance with their lives.' In reporting on the casualties of the war, she may have inadvertently added to the toll. Stack's strong sense of guilt demonstrates that she has learnt a crucial lesson: journalists have a responsibility not to put people in danger for a possible story.

Stack cannot change Ahmed's fate, but she can control the way that she tells his story. Although she never reported it in the media, she does include it in the book. This is revealing: Stack could have kept such an intimate situation, which exposes her to professional scrutiny, to herself. However, with an admirable commitment to truth, she reveals what happened. The details Stack includes give us an insight into who Ahmed was: a passionate athlete with a 'shy grin' and a 'skinny frame', a loyal son in love with a girl causing him angst. In a way, personalising Ahmed may be a form of atonement. In life, Stack may have seen him as a symbol, but on the page she can represent him with the complexity he deserves. However, there is a tension here too, because her encounter with Ahmed does serve a symbolic function in the text. Stack alerts us to this when she identifies herself as 'part of an American plague', thus inviting us to identify Ahmed with Iraq. In this, we may see that although Stack has become aware of the problems of representing individuals caught up in international conflict, she has not found an effective solution to these problems.

Through her encounter with Ahmed, Stack learns much about the nature of journalism and the responsibilities of reporters, which entail both a commitment to the truth and a respect for individuals' lives. Stack feels guilty over Ahmed; yet her interviews with him were part of a genuine endeavour to tell an important story, in the way most likely to affect readers. Her experiences with Ahmed reveal to her – and to us – that in a time of war, a reporter is not simply a witness, but a participant.

REFERENCES & READING

Text

Stack, Megan 2010, *Every Man in This Village Is a Liar*, Scribe Publications, Melbourne.

Books

Filkins, Dexter 2008, *The Forever War*, Vintage, New York.

Finkel, David 2009, *The Good Soldiers*, Scribe Publications, Melbourne.

Herr, Michael 1977, *Dispatches*, Picador, London.

Junger, Sebastian 2010, *War*, Fourth Estate, London.

Interview

'Megan Stack: An Education in War', recorded at the Byron Bay Writers Festival, 6 August 2010, www.abc.net.au/tv/bigideas/stories/2010/08/31/2997267.htm

Newspaper articles

Hamilton, Adrian 2010, '*Every Man in This Village Is a Liar*, by Megan Stack', 10 September, www.independent.co.uk/arts-entertainment/books/reviews/every-man-in-this-village-is-a-liar-by-megan-stack-2075076.html

Shamsie, Kamila 2010, '*Every Man in This Village Is a Liar*: *An Education in War* by Megan Stack', 21 August, www.theguardian.com/books/2010/aug/21/every-man-in-this-village-is-a-liar-megan-stack

Stone, Marla 2010, '*Every Man in This Village Is a Liar* by Megan K. Stack', 20 June, http://articles.latimes.com/2010/jun/20/entertainment/la-ca-megan-stack-20100620